THE MYTH OF MARS AND VENUS

Deborah Cameron

OXFORD
UNIVERSITY PRESS

OXFORD
UNIVERSITY PRESS

Great Clarendon Street, Oxford OX2 6DP

Oxford University Press is a department of the University of Oxford.
It furthers the University's objective of excellence in research, scholarship,
and education by publishing worldwide in
Oxford New York

Auckland Cape Town Dar es Salaam Hong Kong Karachi
Kuala Lumpur Madrid Melbourne Mexico City Nairobi
New Delhi Shanghai Taipei Toronto

With offices in

Argentina Austria Brazil Chile Czech Republic France Greece
Guatemala Hungary Italy Japan Poland Portugal Singapore
South Korea Switzerland Thailand Turkey Ukraine Vietnam

Oxford is a registered trade mark of Oxford University Press
in the UK and in certain other countries

Published in the United States
by Oxford University Press Inc., New York

British Library Cataloguing in Publication Data

Data available

Library of Congress Cataloging in Publication Data

Data available

Typeset in 10.75/15pt Dante by Graphicraft Limited, Hong Kong
Printed in Great Britain by Clays Ltd, St Ives plc

ISBN 978-0-19-921447-1

1

Acknowledgements

The Myth of Mars and Venus has two related goals. One is to dispel some of the myths that currently surround the subject of male–female differences in language and communication. The other is to put something in place of those myths, by making the relevant linguistic research accessible to a wider audience. Some of the research I have drawn on is my own, but much of it is the work of other language and gender scholars. Although they should not be held responsible for the views expressed in this book, it could not have been written without them, and I acknowledge my debt to them with thanks. I am particularly grateful to Penelope Eckert, Susan Ehrlich, Janet Holmes, Don Kulick, Fiona McAlinden, Sally McConnell-Ginet, Miriam Meyerhoff, Kathy O'Leary, Momoko Nakamura, and Sylvia Shaw. I also thank Meryl Altman, Joan Scanlon, and Jane Taubman for their comments, suggestions, and general encouragement, and my editor Ben Harris for his patience.

Contents

1
Myths and Why They Matter

Do men and women speak the same language? Can they ever really communicate? These questions are not new, but since the early 1990s there has been a new surge of interest in them. Countless self-help and popular psychology books have been written portraying men and women as alien beings, and conversation between them as a catalogue of misunderstandings. The most successful exponents of this formula, writers like Deborah Tannen and John Gray, have topped the best-seller lists on both sides of the Atlantic.[1] Advice on how to bridge the communication gulf between the sexes has grown into a flourishing multimedia industry. John Gray's official website, for instance, promotes not only his various 'Mars and Venus' books, but also seminars, residential 'retreats', a telephone helpline, and a dating service.

Readers who prefer something a little harder-edged can turn to a genre of popular science books with titles like *Brain Sex, Sex on the Brain, The Essential Difference*, and *Why Men Don't*

Iron.[2] This literature explains that the gulf between men and women is a product of nature, not nurture. The sexes communicate differently (and women do it better) because of the way their brains are wired. The female brain excels in verbal tasks whereas the male brain is better adapted to visual-spatial and mathematical tasks. Women like to talk, but men prefer action to words.

Writers in this vein are fond of presenting themselves as latter-day Galileos, braving the wrath of the political correctness lobby by daring to challenge the feminist orthodoxy which denies that men and women are by nature profoundly different. Simon Baron-Cohen, the author of *The Essential Difference*, explains in his introduction that he put the book aside for several years because 'the topic was just too politically sensitive'.[3] In the chapter on male–female differences in his book about human nature, *The Blank Slate*, Steven Pinker congratulates himself on having the courage to say what has long been 'unsayable in polite company'.[4] Both writers stress that they have no political axe to grind: they are simply following the evidence where it leads, and trying to put scientific facts in place of politically correct dogma.

Yet before we applaud, we should perhaps pause to ask ourselves: since when has silence reigned about the differences between men and women? Certainly not since the early 1990s, when the previous steady trickle of books began to develop into a raging torrent. By now, a writer who announces that sex-differences are natural is not 'saying the unsayable', he or she is stating the obvious. The proposition that men and women *communicate* differently is particularly uncontroversial, with clichés like 'men never listen' and 'women find it easier to talk about their feelings' referenced constantly in everything from women's magazines to humorous greeting cards. A few years ago, a British Telecom advertisement informed us that men like to conduct phone calls standing up, whereas women prefer to sit down. Even if this were a proven fact (which I doubt it is), the obvious response would be 'so what?' But today we seem willing to treat even the most implausible and trivial claims as worthy of serious attention.

The idea that men and women 'speak different languages' has itself become a dogma, treated not as a hypothesis to be investigated or as a claim to be adjudicated, but as an unquestioned article of faith. In this book I propose to question it, and to argue that our faith in it is misplaced. Like the scientists I have mentioned, I believe in following the evidence where it leads. But in this case, the evidence does not lead where most people think it does. If we examine the findings of more than thirty years of research on language, communication, and the sexes, we will discover that they tell a different, and more complicated, story. That is the story which this book will tell.

I have two reasons for wanting to tell it. One is simply that it is interesting, and deserves to be more widely known. The other, though, is more overtly political. I have called this book *The Myth of Mars and Venus*, and I use the word 'myth' in two senses. The idea that men and women differ fundamentally in the way they use language to communicate is a myth in the everyday sense: a widespread but false belief. But it is also a myth in the sense of being a story people tell in order to explain who they are, where they have come from, and why they live as they do. Whether or not they are 'true' in any historical or scientific sense, such stories have consequences in the real world. They shape our beliefs, and so influence our actions. The myth of Mars and Venus is no exception to that rule.

For example, the belief that 'male–female miscommunication' is an endemic problem is increasingly influencing the way we deal with the crimes of rape and sexual assault. Defence lawyers can now argue that because the sexes communicate differently, a man may genuinely, and through no fault of his own, have understood a woman to be consenting to sex when by her own account she was doing no such thing. If this argument is accepted, the defendant may be acquitted or punished less severely on the grounds that he did not intentionally disregard the woman's wishes, he simply misinterpreted them.

The 'miscommunication' idea is also central to many programmes of sex education designed to reduce the risk of rape. Women are told that because men favour a more direct style of communication, the only kind of refusal that is certain to get through to them is a firm 'no'. As we will see in Chapter 5, linguistic research suggests that this belief is unfounded, and that following advice based on it may actually put women at greater risk of violence.

The workplace is another domain in which myths about language and the sexes can have detrimental effects. A few years ago, the manager of a call centre in north-east England was asked by an interviewer why women made up such a high proportion of the agents he employed. Did men not apply for jobs in his centre? The manager replied that any vacancies he had available attracted numerous applicants of both sexes, since unemployment rates in the area were high. But as he went on to explain: 'We are looking for people who can chat to people, interact, build rapport. What we find is that women can do this more . . . women are naturally good at that sort of thing.' Moments later, he admitted: 'I suppose we do, if we're honest about it, select women sometimes because they are women rather than because of something they've particularly shown in the interview.'[5]

The growth of call centres is part of a larger trend in economically advanced societies. More jobs are now in the service than the manufacturing sector, and service jobs, particularly those that involve direct contact with customers, put a higher premium on language and communication skills. Many employers share the call centre manager's belief that women are by nature better qualified than men for jobs of this kind, and one result is a form of discrimination. Male job applicants have to prove that they possess the necessary skills, whereas women are just assumed to possess them. In today's increasingly service-based economy, this may not be good news for men.

But it is not only men who stand to lose because of the widespread conviction that women have superior verbal skills. Someone else who thinks men and women are naturally suited to different kinds of work is Simon Baron-Cohen: in *The*

Essential Difference he offers the following 'scientific' careers advice.

> People with the female brain make the most wonderful coun-
> sellors, primary school teachers, nurses, carers, therapists, social
> workers, mediators, group facilitators or personnel staff. . . .
> People with the male brain make the most wonderful scientists,
> engineers, mechanics, technicians, musicians, architects, electri-
> cians, plumbers, taxonomists, catalogists, bankers, toolmakers,
> programmers or even lawyers.[6]

The difference between the two lists reflects what Baron-
Cohen takes to be the 'essential difference' between male and
female brains. The female-brain jobs make use of a capacity
for empathy and communication, whereas the male ones
exploit the ability to analyse complex systems. Baron-Cohen is
careful to talk about 'people with the female/male brain'
rather 'men and women'. He stresses that there are men
with female brains, women with male brains, and individuals
of both sexes with 'balanced' brains. He refers to the major
brain-types as 'male' and 'female', however, because the tendency is for males to have male brains and females to have
female brains. And at many points it becomes clear that in
spite of his caveats about not confusing gender with brain-
sex, he himself is doing exactly that.

The passage reproduced above is a good example. Baron-
Cohen classifies nursing as a female-brain, empathy-based job
(though if a caring and empathetic nurse cannot measure
dosages accurately and make systematic clinical observations

she or he risks doing serious harm) and law as a male-brain, system-analysing job (though a lawyer, however well versed in the law, will not get far without communication and people-reading skills). These categorizations are not based on a dispassionate analysis of the demands made by the two jobs. They are based on the everyday common-sense knowledge that most nurses are women and most lawyers are men.

If you read the two lists in their entirety, it is hard not to be struck by another 'essential difference': the male jobs are more varied, more creative, and better rewarded than their female counterparts. Baron-Cohen's job-lists take me back to my schooldays thirty-five years ago, when the aptitude tests we had to complete before being interviewed by a careers adviser were printed on pink or blue paper. In those days we called this sexism, not science.

✴ Mars and Venus: a closer look

At its most basic, what I am calling 'the myth of Mars and Venus' is simply the proposition that men and women differ fundamentally in the way they use language to communicate. All versions of the myth share this basic premiss; most versions, in addition, make some or all of the following claims:

1. Language and communication matter more to women than to men; women talk more than men.

2. Women are more verbally skilled than men.

3. Men's goals in using language tend to be instrumental—about getting things done—whereas women's tend to be

interpersonal or relational—about making connections to other people. Men talk more about things and facts, whereas women talk more about people, relationships, and feelings.

4. Men's way of using language is competitive, reflecting their general interest in acquiring and maintaining status; women's use of language is cooperative, reflecting their preference for equality and harmony. Because of this, men's style of communicating also tends to be more direct and less polite than women's.

5. These differences routinely lead to 'miscommunication' between the sexes, with each sex misinterpreting the other's intentions. This causes problems in contexts where men and women regularly interact, and especially in heterosexual relationships.

Not all writers make every one of the claims just listed. Which ones are emphasized and which are downplayed is often a question of the genre a writer is working in. The idea that women are better communicators than men is strongly emphasized in popular science books, but more muted in self-help texts; conversely, self-help writers tend to foreground the theme of misunderstanding between men and women, whereas popular science writers are less interested in the minutiae of personal relationships.

The most obvious divergence between the two genres concerns the question of 'nature versus nurture'. Popular science books are typically dedicated to the proposition that sex-differences of all kinds have biological rather than social causes. Differences in men's and women's verbal behaviour are thus explained in biological terms. In self-help books, by contrast, the emphasis is less on explaining the causes of difference and more on dealing with its supposed consequences. Some writers come down on the side of nurture, but many prefer to bypass the whole debate. John Gray, for instance, offers only the whimsical tale that gives his book its title—men and women are different because they originally came to earth from different planets.

Yet despite these variations in emphasis and tone, the self-help and scientific versions of the myth are in the end far more similar than different. Even where they disagree about why men and women differ, they take it as axiomatic that significant differences exist, and are largely in agreement on what the differences are. Most also express the same views on what our attitude to them should be: they advocate tolerance and mutual respect. We should not pretend that the differences do not exist, but nor should we make negative judgements on either sex. We should think of men and women as 'different but equal'.

Simon Baron-Cohen, for instance, concludes *The Essential Difference* with a plea for 'society [to] become more accepting of essential differences in the mind',[7] suggesting that a truly equal society would be one which acknowledged and valued diversity. Deborah Tannen, though she rejects the idea of 'essential differences in the mind' (in her view male–female differences are products of social arrangements), is also in favour of the 'different but equal' approach. She argues that sex differences are like ethnic or national differences, and deserve the same respect. Demanding that one sex assimilate to the other's norm would be like treating one culture as the standard for all. The biological determinist and the cultural relativist may travel by different routes, but they end up at the same destination.

If their readers are happy to follow them there, it is presumably because their argument appeals to mainstream liberal values: who is not in favour of tolerance and respect? 'Different but equal', however, has a less than liberal history. Applied to racial groups, it was part of the official ideology of South African apartheid; applied to women, it was an argument popular in the nineteenth century with anti-suffragists who espoused the doctrine of 'separate spheres'. That doctrine held that each sex had its proper sphere of activity and influence: men should exercise authority in the public sphere of politics, government, trade, and the professions, while deferring to the authority of women in the private sphere of the home. Giving women the right to vote alongside men would disrupt this natural order, thrusting women into men's sphere and diminishing the contribution they made in their own.

One problem with this argument is that just calling two spheres equal does not make them so. The same goes for Simon Baron-Cohen's list of suitable occupations for people with male and female brains. What Baron-Cohen propounds in *The Essential Difference* looks very like a twenty-first-century version of the doctrine of separate spheres. He does not say that a woman's place is in the home, but he does suggest there is a natural division of labour whereby men make things, design things, explain things, and decide things while women serve others and take care of their needs.

Today, when older justifications will no longer wash, the notion that women have a natural vocation to care has become closely linked to the myth of Mars and Venus, which says that women have a particular gift for cooperative, rapport-seeking, empathetic communication. Men, by contrast, have no such gift: they are inarticulate, emotionally illiterate, insensitive, and aggressive.

The literature of Mars and Venus is remarkably patronizing towards men. Even when a writer's overt message is 'different but equal', this is often undercut by vignettes of male–female interaction in which the men come off as bullies, petulant toddlers, or Neanderthals sulking in their caves. One (male) contributor to this catalogue of stereotypes goes so far as to call his book *If Men Could Talk*.[8] A book called *If Women Could Think* would be instantly denounced: why do men put up with books that put them on a par with Lassie or Skippy the Bush Kangaroo ('hey, wait a minute—I think he's trying to tell us something!')?

Perhaps men have realized that a reputation for incompetence can sometimes work to your advantage. Like the idea that they are no good at housework, the idea that men are no good at talking serves to exempt them from doing something which many would rather leave to women anyway. (Though we will see later on that it is only some kinds of talking which men would rather leave to women: in many contexts men have no difficulty expressing themselves—indeed, they tend to dominate the conversation.)

This should remind us that the relationship between the sexes is not only about difference, but also about power. The long-standing expectation that women will serve and care for others is not unrelated to their position as the 'second sex'. But in the universe of Mars and Venus, the fact that we (still) live in a male-dominated society—a society in which the sexes are unequal as well as different—is like an elephant in the room that everyone pretends not to notice. Some writers concede that inequalities exist, but present these as the unfortunate result of our failure to 'value diversity'. If we could learn to understand our differences and show proper respect for one another, unfairness would disappear. But when we introduce power into the equation, an alternative possibility suggests itself. Rather than being treated unequally because they are different, men and women may become different because they are treated unequally.

In the mid-1970s, the linguist Robin Lakoff wrote an essay called *Language and Woman's Place* in which she argued that women's distinctive ways of talking both reflected and perpetuated their subordinate social status.[9] She suggested that many characteristics of 'feminine' verbal behaviour, such as hedging (using qualifiers like 'a bit' and 'sort of'), favouring 'empty' adjectives ('lovely') and elaborate colour terms ('lilac' rather than 'purple'), phrasing statements as questions, being 'super-polite' and avoiding taboo language, were really symbolic expressions of deference or powerlessness. They said: 'I'm not being aggressive about this . . .' or 'I know I have no authority to say this . . .'. Lakoff believed that women were caught in a double bind. If they did not use 'women's language', they risked being judged unfeminine; but by using it they risked confirming the belief that women could not express themselves decisively or authoritatively, and were therefore unfit to occupy positions of responsibility. Women had a choice, but whatever choice they made, they paid a price.

Lakoff's essay was written more than thirty years ago, and some of her specific claims about the way women use language have now been abandoned (they were based more on intuition than evidence, and it turned out that research did not support them). But her more general argument, that there is a connection between language-use, gender, and power, still stands. Though few researchers today believe that power differences on their own explain everything (most do not believe that any single factor on its own can explain everything), power is still very much a part of the picture, because the evidence continues to point to it as one important influence on men's and women's use of language.

You would not know this, however, from reading the literature of Mars and Venus. Popular sources are selective in the use they make of research evidence. On one hand they ignore some very consistent research findings, while on the other, some of their claims are not supported by any evidence at all.

But if the picture presented in Mars and Venus books is selective and inaccurate, why do so many people find it convincing? For most readers, especially of self-help and popular psychology, the answer is probably that they judge what they read by how well it seems to fit with their own experience.

Readers of self-help books often praise them by saying that they found the examples of male and female behaviour 'immediately recognizable'. Yet that too is puzzling, for after all, readers have had years of experience observing real men and women having real conversations. Why would they claim to 'recognize' descriptions of behaviour which are based on myth rather than fact?

Actually, this is a common phenomenon: it happens because of the human tendency to rely on stereotypes when processing information about people. Though we often think of stereotyping as something only the ignorant and prejudiced do, the truth is that we all do it to some degree. Many psychologists would argue that stereotypes—generalized representations of what different groups of people are like—are widespread because they fulfil a vital function in human societies. They are short cuts which help us to deal with new people and situations, by reducing the complexity of human behaviour to manageable proportions. But of course, stereotyping has a downside: it can reinforce unjust prejudices, and make us prone to seeing only what we expect or want to see.

✦ The quest for differences (and how it distorts reality)

My father, like many men of his generation, held the belief that women were incompetent drivers. During my teenage years, family car journeys were invariably accompanied by an endless running commentary on how badly the women around us were driving. Eventually I became so irritated by this, I took to scouring passing traffic for counter-examples: women who were driving perfectly well, and men who were driving like idiots.

My father usually conceded that the men were idiots, but not because they were men. Whereas female idiocy was axiomatically caused by femaleness, substandard male drivers were either 'yobbos'—people with no consideration for others on the road or anywhere else—or 'Sunday drivers'—older men whose driving skills were poor because they used their cars only at weekends. As for the women who drove unremarkably, my father seemed surprised when I pointed them out. It was as if he had literally not noticed them until that moment.

At the time I thought my father was exceptional in his ability to make reality fit his preconceptions, but now I know he was not. Psychologists have found in experimental studies that when interpreting situations people typically pay most attention to things that match their expectations, and often fail to register counter-examples. When they are asked to describe someone's behaviour after watching them for a period of time, people recall actions which were 'stereotype consistent' more quickly and easily than actions which were not; they also remember the stereotypical actions for longer. If their attention is drawn specifically to someone's non-stereotypical behaviour, they often explain it by suggesting that the individual concerned is an exceptional case (like my father's yobbos and Sunday drivers). Stereotypical behaviour, on the other hand, is not considered to need any explanation.[10]

It is not hard to see how these tendencies might lead readers of Mars and Venus books to 'recognize' generalizations about the way men and women use language, provided those generalizations fit with already familiar stereotypes. An anecdote illustrating the point that, say, men are competitive and women cooperative conversationalists will prompt readers to recall the many occasions on which they have observed men competing and women cooperating—while not recalling the occasions, perhaps equally numerous, on which they have observed the opposite. If counter-examples do come to mind ('what about Janet? She's the most competitive person I know'), it is open to readers to apply the classic strategy of putting them in a separate category of exceptions ('of course, she grew up with three brothers / is the only woman in her department / works in a particularly competitive business').

In relation to men and women, our most basic stereotypical expectation is simply that they will be different rather than the same. We actively look for differences, and seek out sources which discuss them. Faced with claims like BT's 'men stand up to make phone calls whereas women sit down', our first reaction is more likely to be 'how interesting' than 'what nonsense' or 'who cares?' We are much less attentive to, and less interested in hearing about, similarities between men and women. And this has consequences, not only for our everyday conversations, but also for what goes on in the supposedly more objective realm of science.

Most research studies investigating the behaviour of men and women are designed around the question: 'is there a difference?'—and the presumption is usually that there will be. If a study finds a significant difference between male and female subjects (in other words, a result which statistical tests show could not have been produced by chance), that is considered to be a 'positive' finding, and has a good chance of being published in a scientific journal. A study which finds no significant differences is less likely to be published. This means that some negative findings are never even submitted for publication. It also means that if a study has examined a large number of variables and found positive results for only one or two of them, it will be the least typical, positive findings which the researchers emphasize.

The preference for positive findings is on one level understandable. A report which says, in essence, 'we looked for something and didn't find it' does not make for compelling reading. But if the research was competently designed and carried out, whatever it finds must surely count as knowledge. 'Men and women did not perform any differently on task X' is no less a fact than 'men and women performed significantly differently on task X'. If findings that confirm male–female differences get published more often than findings that disconfirm those differences, the resulting research literature will systematically distort the picture.

✦ Soundbite science

Most people, of course, do not read academic journals: they get their information about scientific research findings from the reports that appear in newspapers, or from TV science documentaries. These sources often feature research on male–female differences, since media producers know that there is interest in the subject. But the criteria producers use when deciding which studies to report and how to present them introduce another layer of distortion.

In 2005 a study published in the scientific journal *NeuroImage* was picked up by the media all over the world. The following report was typical:

MEN DO HAVE TROUBLE HEARING WOMEN: RESEARCH

Men who are accused of never listening by women now have an excuse—women's voices are more difficult for men to listen to than other men's.

Reports say researchers at Sheffield University in northern England have discovered startling differences in the way the brain responds to male and female sounds.

The research shows men decipher female voices using the auditory part of the brain that processes music, while male voices engage a simpler mechanism.[11]

This is a classic piece of 'soundbite science': a single piece of research making headlines because of the ease with which it can be boiled down to a simple, arresting, and yet familiar proposition. The Sheffield study appears to confirm the truth of a well-worn stereotype (that men don't listen when women talk); it then goes on to supply the kind of explanation that many people expect and want (it's to do with the way men's brains work). This enables the study to be framed as settling an age-old dispute in the ongoing 'battle of the sexes'. As the report I have quoted puts it, men 'now have an excuse'.[12] Contrary to what women may think, men who appear not to be listening to them are not being inconsiderate, they have genuine difficulty hearing what women say. If the researchers had found that men's brains processed male and female speech in exactly the same way, that would also have contributed something to the sum of human knowledge. But we can be pretty sure the media would not have been interested in reporting it.

At least in this case the media were reporting a genuine research finding that had been published in a peer-reviewed journal. But there are cases where the headlines trumpet so-called facts which turn out on investigation to have no basis in evidence at all. In 2006, for instance, a popular science book called *The Female Brain* claimed that women on average utter 20,000 words a day, while men on average utter only 7,000.[13] Like 'men have trouble hearing women', this was perfect material for soundbite science: it confirmed the popular belief that women are the more talkative sex, while also suggesting that the magnitude of the difference was even greater than anyone had previously imagined. The 'fact' that women talk nearly three times as much as men was reported in newspapers around the world.

One person who found it impossible to believe was Mark Liberman, a professor of phonetics who has worked extensively with recorded speech. His scepticism prompted him to delve into the footnotes of *The Female Brain* to find out where the author had got her figures. What he found was not an academic citation but a reference to a self-help book. Following the trail into the thickets of popular literature, Liberman came across several competing statistical claims. The figures varied wildly: different authors (and sometimes even the same author in different books) gave average female daily word-counts ranging from 4,000 to 25,000 words. As far as Liberman could tell, all these numbers were plucked from thin air: in no case did anyone cite any actual research to back them up. He concluded that no one had ever done a study counting the words produced by a sample of men and women in the course of a single day. The claims were so variable because they were pure guesswork.[14]

After Liberman pointed this out in a newspaper article,[15] the author of *The Female Brain* conceded that her claim was not supported by evidence and said it would be deleted from future editions. But the damage was already done: the much-publicized soundbite that women talk three times as much as men will linger in people's memories and get recycled in their conversations, whereas the little-publicized retraction will make no such impression. This is how myths acquire the status of facts.

My goal in this book is not to deny that there are any differences between men and women, nor to suggest that people should not be interested in those differences. Rather, my goal is to separate facts from myths, evidence from anecdote, and reasonable conclusions from speculative and sweeping generalizations. If we are serious about understanding the relationship between language and gender, we need more sophisticated ways of thinking about men and women, their similarities and their differences. The myth of Mars and Venus is crude and reductive: it both exaggerates the extent of the differences and oversimplifies the reasons for them.

I am also going to argue that this matters, in ways that are not just 'academic'. I think we ought to be asking three questions about the myth of Mars and Venus. First, what is the evidence for its claims about men, women, and language? Second, what consequences does it have in the real world if large numbers of people believe those claims? And third, why are the claims being made? In an age not only of unprecedented sexual equality, but also of extraordinary advances in scientists' ability to manipulate 'nature'—the age of artificial reproduction and genetic engineering—why are we being so relentlessly exhorted to 'become more accepting' of natural sex-differences? In this book I will try to find answers to those questions.

2

A Time and a Place:
Putting Myths in Context

In 1950, the problem page of *Woman's Own* printed a letter from a woman who complained that her husband was more interested in his hobbies than he was in talking to his wife.[1] The magazine's agony aunt replied:

> I am sorry you are unhappy but I doubt if you will ever really cure your husband of his 'maleness', which is the real trouble. Nature shaped the human male to romp about with his hunting and his war games (in your husband's case watered down to scouting and football) while the female remained in the cave to look after the children.

Another letter published in the same year came from a woman who had started to suspect that her husband did not love her. He was, she said, a good provider and handy about the house, but he never said anything to suggest he was fond of her. The agony aunt reassured her that she was worrying unnecessarily:

> The explanation is that your husband, like so many men, just cannot demonstrate his affection in those small ways that mean so much to most women. The average man feels that by working hard for his wife and children, by doing things about the house and by handing over the best part of his salary, he is expressing his love, as indeed he is in his own way. I suggest you try to accept everything he does for you as being his own particular expression of his love.

This advice from 1950 contains the same basic ingredients that Deborah Tannen and John Gray would later turn into a best-selling formula: unhappy women who crave intimate communication, inarticulate men who are unable to provide it, and experts who urge women to accept what cannot be changed. Evidently the myth of Mars and Venus did not just emerge out of nowhere in the early 1990s. Has it always existed, in some form or other?

The short answer is no: beliefs on this subject are not time-less and universal. They vary across cultures and change over time. But something more abstract does remain constant. In any given time and place, popular beliefs about the language of men and women will be derived from beliefs about men and women themselves—their natures, their relationship to one another, and the places they should occupy in society. As ideas about those things vary and change, so do ideas about the way men and women communicate.

✴ Mars and Venus in history

The current myth of Mars and Venus depends heavily on the idea that whereas women like to talk and are skilled in the verbal arts, men are like the husbands in the problem page letters: they prefer doing to talking, and find it difficult to express themselves in words. In 'scientific' versions of the myth, the explanation given for this is that women's verbal abilities are innately superior to men's. Language skills are said to develop more rapidly in girls; women are described as more articulate and fluent than men, with more extensive vocabularies (from which they retrieve words more quickly) and a greater range of communication styles. They are also said to use language more 'correctly' and more 'politely' than men.

Accurate or not (I will consider the evidence later), these claims have become sufficiently familiar that if you asked a random sample of people 'which sex is more articulate/ fluent/correct/polite?'—or just 'which sex is better with language and communication?'—a majority (of both sexes) would be likely to say 'women'. But that is a relatively recent development. In the not so far-off days when most people thought women were intellectually inferior to men, they also believed women were linguistically inferior.

A good place to begin this excursion into history is in eighteenth-century England. The eighteenth century was a period of intense concern about the proper use of language, and is therefore a rich source of evidence about the attitudes people held. Commentators emphasized the linguistic virtues of eloquence, politeness, and correctness, while worrying about the 'corruption' of language by their opposites. And it was men (or more exactly, men of the elite class) who were regarded as more eloquent, more polite, and more correct. Men were the guardians of linguistic propriety, whereas women's shortcomings threatened constantly to corrupt it. Those shortcomings were a regular target for criticism and satire. Here, for instance, is Lord Chesterfield's sarcastic assessment, made in 1777:

> Language is indisputably the more immediate province of the fair sex: there they shine, there they excel. The torrents of their eloquence, especially in the vituperative way, stun all opposition, and bear away, in one promiscuous heap, nouns, verbs, moods and tenses. If words are wanting, which indeed happens but seldom, indignation instantly makes new ones; and I have often known four or five syllables that never met one another before, hastily and fortuitously jumbled into some word of mighty import.[2]

One of Chesterfield's stereotypes is still recognizable: that women talk too much. But in other respects his beliefs are remote from those which are commonplace today. Women are not cooperative, they are 'vituperative'. Their vocabularies are not more extensive than men's, but on the contrary, so impoverished that they must resort to making up words by jumbling syllables together. Grammatical correctness is not their strong point either: their combined loquacity and ignorance causes them to mix up 'nouns, verbs, moods and tenses'.

Because we have no direct evidence about the way men and women *spoke* in Chesterfield's time—we are dependent on written sources, the vast majority of them writing by men—it is difficult to know whether this description of women's speech (which is echoed by numerous other commentators of the period) reflects reality or simply prejudice. That there was prejudice is obvious to anyone who reads contemporary sources. But it is also possible that many women in eighteenth-century England really did have less extensive vocabularies and a less secure grasp of 'correct' usage than men (that is, men of the elite class). Women generally received less education than men, and were educated in English rather than studying Latin and Greek as men did. (Many rules of correct English usage in the eighteenth century were based on Latin rules, and many complex words were borrowed from Latin.)

One slightly earlier commentator, the anonymous female author of *An Essay in Defence of the Female Sex*, had denied that women were linguistically disadvantaged by their lack of classical education. On the contrary, she suggested, *not* having to spend years mastering Latin gave girls a head start on English: their 'command of words and sense' was developed by reading books in their own language from an early age. Boys, she said, lagged many years behind, and 'at Seventeen or Eighteen are . . . but where the Girles were at Nine or Ten'.[3]

This writer's view was, however, an unusual one for her time. It was only later that women became by common consent the linguistically superior sex. Particularly in areas of verbal behaviour that were thought to reflect more general intellectual abilities, men were still being described as superior to women well into the twentieth century.

In 1922, the Danish scholar Otto Jespersen published a general survey of the nature and origins of language, which included a chapter called 'The Woman'. Drawing on sources as diverse (and in some cases as unreliable) as seventeenth-century travellers' tales, the dialogue given to women characters by male novelists and dramatists, his own observations, and experiments conducted by psychologists, Jespersen attempted to summarize what was known at the time about male–female differences in language-use.

'The Woman' is one of the earliest sources to take a systematic and scientific approach to this topic: Jespersen was clearly striving for a 'balanced' assessment. But to a modern reader it is clear that he was biased: he considered women less logical and creative thinkers than men, and took it for granted that their use of language must reflect that.

Jespersen does praise women for the civilizing influence they exert on the development of languages through what he calls 'their instinctive shrinking from coarse and gross expressions and their preference for refined . . . veiled and indirect expressions'.[4] He follows this, however, by noting that 'there is a danger of the language becoming languid and insipid if we are always to content ourselves with women's expressions'.[5] Chesterfield, writing in an age that considered innovations in language to be 'corruptions', had attributed the habit of making up new words to women; Jespersen, writing in an age that valued originality and inventiveness, says that men are responsible for 'renovating' language by coining new words.

One belief Jespersen shares with eighteenth-century commentators, but not with the experts of today, is that women have smaller vocabularies than men. He describes one research study in which the experimenter asked twenty-five male and twenty-five female students to write down as quickly as possible the first 100 words that came into their heads. The men produced about 250 more words than the women, and more of the men's words were abstract terms. Jespersen comments that women's vocabulary is both less extensive and more 'everyday' than men's. His explanation is connected to a theory that had been advanced by educationalists in the nineteenth century: women's minds are quick but shallow, whereas men think more slowly but also more deeply:

> Woman is linguistically quicker than man: quicker to hear, quicker to learn and quicker to answer. A man is slower: he hesitates, he chews the cud to make sure of the taste of words . . . thus preparing himself for the appropriate use of the fittest noun or adjective.[6]

The shallowness of women's minds is also apparent in the way they construct their sentences. According to Jespersen, men use subordinate clauses to express logical relationships between ideas, whereas women simply string the ideas together with the all-purpose conjunction *and*—'the gradation between the respective ideas being marked not grammatically, but emotionally, by stress and intonation, and in writing by underlining'.[7] Incomplete and exclamatory sentences (like 'well I never!') are also described as characteristic of women. Explaining this, Jespersen quotes the novelist Thomas Hardy, who once described a female character as 'that novelty among women—one who finished a thought before beginning the sentence that was to convey it'.

To a contemporary reader, the comments I have quoted from Jespersen are likely to seem at best condescending to women, and at worst downright offensive. But in his time, Jespersen would not have stood out as especially prejudiced. His prejudices were uncontroversial, accepted by most people as obvious common sense. The problem we have with them now reflects the fact that common sense has changed.

The biggest change is that we no longer believe women are less intelligent, rational, or logical than men. We are therefore reluctant to swallow linguistic stereotypes derived from that proposition, such as the idea that women cannot form grammatically complex sentences. Other, less unflattering stereotypes—like the idea that women are more refined and less 'coarse' in their language than men—have fared better. And a few of the old criticisms, for instance that women talk excessively and are overemotional, have not only survived, they have been recast in positive terms. Today, 'articulacy' or 'fluency' and 'emotional literacy' are among the qualities that are considered to make women better communicators than men.

This reflects another big change in our thinking, not only about men and women but also about language and communication. There has been a shift in what kinds of speech we consider most valuable or most skilful. The historian Theodore Zeldin observes that Victorian advice on how to talk to others is strong on matters of etiquette, but leaves out something modern readers regard as far more important: 'the idea of personal contact, of the intimate meeting of minds and sympathies'.[8] Since Victorian times (and especially since the rise of 'therapy culture' in the 1960s and 1970s), enabling this 'intimate meeting of minds' has come to be understood as the essence of good communication. Consequently, the modern understanding of verbal 'skill' puts less emphasis on qualities like eloquence and correctness, and far more on qualities like honesty, sincerity, and empathy.

This shift in our priorities has contributed to the shift in our assessment of men's and women's verbal skills. Eloquence was from Mars, but empathy is from Venus. Or at least, this is how we see things in modern western societies. What, though, about the rest of planet Earth?

✶ Mars and Venus across cultures

In the first half of the twentieth century, a number of anthropologists published descriptions of non-European cultures in which, allegedly, there were distinct men's and women's languages. The scholars did not mean that the sexes used completely different linguistic systems, but that there were differences in the word-forms they used or in their pronunciations of certain sounds. For instance, Alexander Chamberlain, in a brief note on 'Women's Languages' published in 1912, says that among the Caraya Indians, the name of a drink called *jacuba* is pronounced *šăúbă* by men and *šăkúbă* by women.[9]

This interest in 'women's languages' was part of a more general preoccupation with the 'exotic' and the 'primitive'. Variant linguistic forms for men and women were regarded as survivals from an earlier stage of human cultural development, which had long since disappeared from the most advanced civilizations. In 1944, Paul Furfey referred to sexual differentiation in language as 'a phenomenon which is barely discernable in the familiar languages of Europe, but which is not at all uncommon among primitive peoples'.[10] He also suggested that it was 'a tool of [male] sex-dominance'.

Commentators like Furfey equated the levelling out of linguistic sex-differences, which they claimed had taken place in European cultures, with civilization and social progress: extensive marking of sex-differences in speech was for them a sign of backwardness. This casts an interesting sidelight on the current popularity of the myth of Mars and Venus. However, we now know these early scholars were wrong to see sexual differentiation in language-use as something confined to traditional non-western cultures: similar patterns are found in western speech communities too. Their perception of sex-differences as alien and exotic led them to exaggerate the distinctiveness of the male and female speech-forms they reported, and perhaps to misconstrue the meaning of the differences.

Like the concept of 'primitive peoples' to which it was connected, the idea of 'men's and women's languages' is no longer
current among linguistic anthropologists. But research on
how gender influences ways of speaking in different cultures
has continued: its findings underline the point that Mars and
Venus generalizations about men's and women's language do
not have universal applicability.

In Gapun, a remote village on the Sepik River in Papua New
Guinea, Jespersen's observation that women 'instinctive[ly]
shrink from coarse and gross expressions' would be greeted
with incomprehension if not derision. In this community,
coarse and gross expressions are something of a female
speciality. When Gapun women get annoyed with their husbands (or indeed with anyone else, though their husbands are
in practice the commonest targets) they do not ventilate their
grievances to the local equivalent of an agony aunt. They do it
by way of a speech genre that is known in the village as a *kros*.

A *kros*—the word means 'angry' in Tok Pisin[11]—is a
monologue in which one person complains about another's
behaviour, generally in highly abusive terms, and often at
considerable length (forty-five minutes is not unusual). It is
delivered from inside the speaker's own house, but is intended
to be heard by the entire village. The rule is that the target may
not answer back, and nor may anyone else on their behalf. If
the *kros* turns from a monologue into an argument, there is a
good chance it will soon degenerate into a physical fight.
Gapuners prefer to let the speaker go on until she feels she has
said all she needs to say. Her grievance, now a matter of public

record, can if necessary be addressed later through more diplomatic channels.

I have used the pronouns *she* and *her* in this description because the *kros*, almost without exception, is a women's genre. (Widowers may occasionally have a *kros*; other men who feel the need generally get their wives to do it for them.) In one *kros* recorded by the anthropologist Don Kulick, the speaker, Sake, turns on her husband, Allan, after an altercation which begins when Sake falls through a hole in the rotten floor of her house (a house which Allan built, and is in theory responsible for maintaining). In the ensuing conflict Allan hits Sake with a piece of sugar cane, while she threatens to slice him up with a machete and then burn the house to the ground. When Allan leaves the house, Sake begins a tirade of abuse. The following (translated) extract gives the flavour of it:[12]

> You're a fucking rubbish man. You hear? Your fucking prick is full of maggots. You're a big fucking semen prick. Stone balls! . . . Fucking black prick! Fucking grandfather prick! You've built me a good house that I just fall down in, you get up and hit me on the arm with a piece of sugar cane! You fucking mother's cunt!

It is true, of course, that an anthropologist would probably be able to record women using similarly obscene language in any British town centre after closing time on a Friday night. But when western women behave in this way, they are usually considered to be adopting 'masculine' traits. In Gapun, by contrast, women whose language is direct, aggressive, abusive, and obscene are not thought to be acting like men. They are thought to be doing what comes naturally to women.

Villagers hold the general belief that human beings are endowed with two opposing qualities, known as *hed* (roughly, being wilful or headstrong) and *save* (literally, 'knowledge', but what is meant by it here is more like 'judgement' or 'good sense'). *Hed* is something people are born with; *save* takes time to develop. But while every adult has both, men are more able than women to subordinate *hed* to *save*, and that difference is manifested in their verbal behaviour. Men pride themselves on their ability to express themselves indirectly, controlling their emotions and concealing their real opinions to avoid provoking conflict. Women on the other hand are uncooperative and belligerent. As Kruni, one of the older men in the village, told Don Kulick: 'They don't suppress their *hed* a little bit. No way. Talk *kros*, bad talk, that's the way of the women, their habit. They don't have any *save*.'[13]

In John Gray's terms, Gapun would seem to be a place where men are from Venus and women are from Mars. And Gapun is not the only such place. The precise form women's Martian behaviour takes in Gapun is specific to Gapun, but the distinction made in the village between women's direct and adversarial style of speaking and men's more indirect, consensus-seeking style has parallels elsewhere.

Elinor Ochs Keenan encountered a similar distinction while doing ethnographic work among the Malagasy people of Madagascar. In this society, the norm of maintaining harmonious social relations is particularly strong. Open confrontation is severely frowned on, and even such ordinary actions as asking someone a direct question are considered impolite, because they are seen as putting the addressee too much on the spot. There is an extremely formal and indirect traditional style of speaking called *kabary*, which is used on ritual occasions. *Kabary* is highly valued—and only men are considered capable of using it. As Keenan explains,

> Men tend not to express their sentiments openly. They admire others who use language subtly. They behave in public in such a way as to promote interpersonal ease. In short, they avoid creating unpleasant face-to-face encounters. Women, on the other hand, tend to speak in a more straightforward manner. They express feelings of anger or criticism directly to the relevant party. Both men and women agree that women have *lavalela*, a long tongue. . . . They consider the use of speech by men to be more skilful than that by women.[14]

Keenan goes on to observe that Malagasy men (rather like the men in Gapun who get their wives to have a *kros* on their behalf) exploit women's linguistic 'deficiencies' when it suits their purposes to do so. They leave it to women to communicate unwelcome information, issue reprimands, request favours, and ask direct questions like 'where have you been?' or 'what did that cost?' They also give women primary responsibility for buying and selling in the local markets. An extremely indirect way of communicating is not an advantage when you are competing to sell your wares and haggling over prices. Malagasy women thus dominate one economically important sphere of activity: but it does not have the same cultural value, or the same political influence, as the male sphere of formal and ritual oratory.

According to the ethnographer Joel Sherzer, the two cases just discussed exemplify a common pattern ('not universal, but certainly widespread') in traditional non-western societies. Many of these societies, he says, recognize two distinct styles of speech:

> indirect, allusive and metaphorical speech, which is highly valued by the society in a socio-aesthetic sense and is also associated with men, politics and the public domain, and direct, non-allusive speech, which is not valued by the society in a socio-aesthetic sense and is associated with women.[15]

Traditional oratory is often both indirect and highly ritualized, making use of stories, proverbs, incantations, and other special ways of speaking that have been passed down through the generations. These features distinguish formal and ceremonial speech from everyday speech, and being able to deploy them appropriately is the mark of a 'skilled' speaker. Often, this kind of verbal skill is a prerequisite for political influence and leadership within the community. But it is almost always men who are believed to possess the relevant skills, and who monopolize positions of leadership.

✴ Mars and Venus in the modern West

Different though they are in substance, the beliefs I have cited from different times and different cultures do have one thing in common. Whatever is said to be typical of women's speech is also said to make women less well suited than men to occupy positions of power and authority. In traditional societies which value indirect, consensus-seeking speech-styles, those styles are associated with men: women are considered too direct to make good leaders. In the West, where public and leadership roles have been seen to demand direct and assertive ways of speaking, it has also been men who were thought to possess the necessary verbal skills, while women were considered insufficiently direct.

It used to be a common argument, for instance, that women did not reach the top ranks of business and the professions because they lacked verbal authority and confidence. Many commentators on the under-representation of women in British parliamentary politics have suggested that this is partly explained by women's inability to deal with the extremely adversarial style of debate for which the House of Commons is famous. But I am choosing my verb tenses carefully here, for it does seem that recently things have been changing.

In 1997, when the landslide general election victory of Tony Blair's New Labour party sent a record number of women MPs to Westminster, some commentators did ask: 'how on earth are they going to cope?' But a different reaction was more common: the view that women's presence should be welcomed, not in spite of their less sharply honed debating skills, but because of them. Women would improve the quality of political debate by making the House of Commons, in one journalist's words, 'less of a bear garden'.[16]

The journalist did not mean merely that women would exercise a restraining influence on men's 'coarseness'. The idea was rather that women would introduce a whole new style of political discourse. As newly elected Labour MP Julia Drown remarked, 'women are more cooperative . . . They're not so into scoring points, and more interested in hearing different points of view.' Her colleague Gisela Stuart concurred, adding that 'democracy is about consensus rather than imposing will'.

Skilled exponents of adversarial politics, like Winston Churchill and Margaret Thatcher ('the lady's not for turning'), presumably did not think that arguing with or 'scoring points' against political opponents was inimical to democracy. Nor did the ancient Greeks who gave us the word. But this is the age of Venus: we are constantly told that the modern way to get things done is through cooperation, negotiation, motivation, and teamwork. These are buzzwords in business as well as in politics. 'The best new managers', proclaimed management guru Tom Peters in 1990, 'will listen, motivate, support.' He went on to pose the obvious rhetorical question: 'isn't that just like a woman?'[17]

Ours may be the first time and place in history to hold such unequivocally positive beliefs about women's ways of speaking. Whereas eighteenth-century writers openly disparaged women, and early twentieth-century commentators like Jespersen damned them with faint praise (their speech was quick but shallow, and polite but 'insipid'), we in the twenty-first century congratulate women unreservedly on their verbal skills. We are also far more ready than our predecessors to find fault with men's.

Is this a sign of progress? In some ways, perhaps: but we should be cautious about drawing the conclusion that where 'they' were prejudiced, 'we' are enlightened. It is always much easier to notice the prejudices of other times and other cultures than it is to examine our own beliefs with a critical eye. But the very fact that beliefs on this subject have been so variable might suggest that a degree of scepticism is in order. If male–female linguistic differences are rooted in biology, as so many contemporary scientists assert, why do different societies claim to observe diametrically opposed patterns of difference? Why are westerners convinced that women are more cooperative and more attentive to others' feelings than men, while in New Guinea and Madagascar people are equally convinced that the reverse is true? And if female verbal superiority is a scientific fact, why have so many cultures, for most of recorded history, considered men's verbal skills (however these were described) to be more advanced than women's?

These are questions I will return to later on. Meanwhile, they should remind us that beliefs about male–female differences are never neutral. When we read Chesterfield or Jespersen now, it is obvious that they were participating, and taking sides, in an ongoing cultural conversation about the roles of men and women in society. Even if it is less obvious, the same is true of today's commentators.

Approaching our own beliefs in a critical spirit means inquiring into the reasons for the current popularity of certain ideas (and the unpopularity of others). It also means investigating the practical consequences of their popularity. (We will see later, for instance, that notwithstanding the predictions of Tom Peters et al., women in business and politics do not seem to be benefiting from their much-vaunted verbal skills.) Most of all, though, it means asking the question: are we justified in believing what we do? Are our beliefs based on evidence, and is that evidence convincing? In the next chapter I will begin to explain why many researchers today do not think so.

3

Partial Truths:

Why Difference is not
the Whole Story

In 2005, an article appeared in the journal *American Psycho-logist* with the title 'The Gender Similarities Hypothesis'.[1] This title stood out as unusual, because the aim of most research studies is to find differences rather than similarities between men and women. Yet as the article's author Janet S. Hyde pointed out, on closer inspection the results of these studies very often show more similarity than difference.

Hyde is a psychologist who specializes in 'meta-analysis', a statistical technique which allows the analyst to collate many different research findings and draw overall conclusions from them. Unlike the media, whose science stories typically revolve around a single eye-catching finding, scientists believe that one study on its own does not show anything: results are only considered reliable if a number of different studies have replicated them. In any field of inquiry, the published literature will contain numerous studies of the same question, and since their findings will usually be mixed rather than uniform, it is necessary to make an assessment of what overall trend, if any, they reveal.

Suppose that the question is 'who interrupts more, men or women?' Some studies will have found that men interrupt more, others that women do, and others may have found no significant difference. In some studies the reported gender difference will be large, while in others it will be much smaller. The number of people whose behaviour was investigated will also vary from study to study. Meta-analysis enables you to aggregate the various results, controlling for things that make them difficult to compare directly, and calculate the overall effect of gender on interruption.

Hyde used this technique to review a large number of studies concerned with all kinds of putative male–female differences—everything from how far men and women can throw to how willing they are to have casual sex. In Table 1, I have extracted the results for just those studies that dealt with gender differences in linguistic and communicative behaviour.

To read this table you need to know that d is the formula indicating the size of the overall gender difference: minus values for d indicate that females are ahead of males, whereas plus values indicate that males are ahead of females. So for instance, the table tells us that when the findings of different studies are aggregated, the overall conclusion is that men interrupt more than women and women self-disclose more than men. However, the really interesting information is in the last column, which tells us whether the actual figure given for d indicates an effect that is very large, large, moderate, small, or close to zero. In almost every case, the overall difference made by gender is either small or close to zero. Two items, spelling accuracy and frequency of smiling, show a larger effect—but it is still only moderate, not large.

There were a few areas in which Hyde did find that the effect of gender was large or very large. For instance, studies of aggression and of how far people can throw things have shown a considerable gap between the sexes (men are more aggressive and can throw further). But in studies of verbal

Table 1. Findings of meta-analysis for studies of gender differences in verbal/communicative behaviour

Focus of research	No. of studies analysed	Value of d	Effect size
Reading comprehension	23	-0.06	Close to zero
Vocabulary	44	$-0.02-+0.06$	Close to zero
Spelling	5*	-0.45	Moderate
Verbal reasoning	5*	-0.02	Close to zero
Speech production	12	-0.33	Small
Conversational interruption	70	$+0.15-+0.33$	Small
Talkativeness	73	-0.11	Small
Assertive speech	75	$+0.11$	Small
Affiliative speech	46	-0.26	Small
Self disclosure	205	-0.18	Small
Smiling	418	-0.40	Moderate

Note: asterisks indicate cases where the small number of studies analysed is compensated for by the fact that they were conducted with very large controlled samples.
Source: adapted from Hyde, 'The Gender Similarities Hypothesis'.

abilities and behaviour, the differences between men and women were slight.

This is not a new observation. In 1988 Hyde and her colleague Marcia Linn carried out a meta-analysis of research dealing specifically with gender differences in verbal ability.[2] The conclusion they came to was that the difference between men and women amounted to 'about one tenth of one standard deviation'—statistician-speak for 'negligible'. Another scholar who has considered this question, the linguist Jack Chambers, suggests that the degree of non-overlap in the abilities of male and female speakers in any given population is 'about a quarter of one percent'. It follows that 'for any array of verbal abilities found in an individual woman, there will almost certainly be a man with exactly the same array'.[3]

Chambers's reference to *individual* men and women points to another problem with generalizations like 'men interrupt more than women' or 'women are more talkative than men'. As well as underplaying their similarities, statements of the form 'women do this and men do that' disguise the extent of the variation that exists *within* each gender group. Explaining why he had reacted with instant scepticism to the claim that women talk three times as much as men, phonetician Mark Liberman predicted: 'Whatever the average female versus male difference turns out to be, it will be small compared to the variation among women and among men.'[4] This prediction is based on experience: for many linguistic variables, there is at least as much variation within each gender group as there is between the two. Focusing on the differences between groups while ignoring the differences within them is extremely misleading—but unfortunately, all too common.

Statistics undoubtedly have their uses, but in language and communication research they have to be used with care. Another problem with studies that just count how many times men interrupted and how many times women interrupted in a conversation is that they take linguistic behaviour out of its context. And linguistic behaviour is only meaningful in context. Most of the things we do with language are capable of communicating some range of meanings: it is the context that enables us to interpret what is being communicated in any particular case.

In context, for instance, interrupting someone may be rude or domineering behaviour—a way of silencing and belittling them—or it may be supportive behaviour, signalling enthusiasm for what they are saying. If we take no account of what interruptions mean, simply counting how many men or women produce will not tell us what any difference signifies. In theory, too, this kind of decontextualized counting could actually *conceal* a significant difference—for instance, what if men and women produced similar numbers of interruptions, but men's were mostly used to silence others whereas women's were mostly used to support others?

To make sense of linguistic behaviour, we need to go back to the context and look at what a particular linguistic feature was actually being used to communicate. But when we do this, we may discover that what appear to be gender differences are only indirectly to do with gender—that between gender and language-use there is a 'missing link'.

✴: Missing links

In Chapter 1 I mentioned Robin Lakoff's essay *Language and Woman's Place*, in which she introduced the concept of a distinctive and symbolically powerless 'women's language'.[5] One of the claims Lakoff made about women's language had to do with a grammatical construction called the 'tag question'. A tag question is a statement with a question tagged onto the end of it, like 'it's a nice day today, isn't it?', 'You haven't forgotten, have you?', or 'I'll have dinner ready at six, OK?' Lakoff suggested that women used tag questions more frequently than men. Both sexes, she said, used tag questions for checking information they were uncertain of ('the meeting's at 3.30, right?'), but women also used them in a way that men generally did not: to seek others' approval when expressing their opinions ('it's a nice day') or announcing their plans ('I'll have dinner ready at six').

Lakoff's ideas about women's language were based on her own intuitions rather than systematic research, but her claims prompted other researchers to go out looking for evidence. There were many studies which counted the incidence of tag questions in the speech of men and women, and many of these concluded that Lakoff was wrong: women did not use more tag questions than men. But in this early research the question of what men's or women's tag questions actually communicated was often overlooked. All the researchers did was count them.

In 1984, the question of what tag questions meant in context was addressed in a study by the linguist Janet Holmes.[6] Holmes's data supported Lakoff's claim that one function of tag questions was to check information which the speaker was uncertain of, and Holmes also found—as Lakoff would have predicted—that this was their most common function in the speech of the men in her sample. But she did not agree with Lakoff about the meaning of tag questions that were *not* being used to check information.

Lakoff had suggested that the function of these tags was to seek approval, and the reason women used more of them was insecurity or lack of confidence in their own opinions. Holmes, however, concluded that in most cases their function was to give the person being addressed an opportunity to speak. When someone said, for instance, 'this is a lovely room, isn't it?' what they were communicating was not: 'I'm not sure if I really think the room is lovely', but rather 'this is what I think, and now it's your turn to say what you think'. Holmes called this kind of tag question 'facilitative', because it was used to facilitate the participation of other speakers in a conversation. She found that women used facilitative tag questions more often than men, but in her view this had nothing to do with women lacking confidence. Rather, she suggested that it reflected women's preference for a cooperative style of interaction in which everyone was actively encouraged to contribute.

A couple of years later, the researcher Kathy O'Leary investigated the use of tag questions in professional settings.[7] O'Leary's data came from television talk shows, interaction between teachers and pupils in the classroom, and a radio phone-in show where callers sought medical advice from a doctor. She found that the speaker's role in the interaction was a better predictor of tag-question use than their gender. It was the professional participants (presenters, teachers, or doctors) who used most tag questions, and these tended to be of the facilitative type. Audience members, pupils, and callers used fewer tag questions, and when they did use them, they tended to be the information-checking kind.

The reason for this is fairly obvious. TV presenters, teachers, and doctors are all professional facilitators: their job involves getting other people to talk by asking them questions. Audience members, patients, and pupils, on the other hand, do not have a reciprocal responsibility to get the professionals to talk. Their role is to respond to questions: if they ask any questions themselves it is more likely to be to check they have understood something, ask for additional information, or seek reassurance.

Kathy O'Leary's findings back up Janet Holmes's argument that using tag questions is not a sign of insecurity or powerlessness. In O'Leary's study it was the speakers who had the highest status and the most control over the proceedings who used tag questions most. But O'Leary's results did not straightforwardly support Holmes's suggestion that using facilitative tag questions reflects a female preference for supportive ways of interacting. When men were playing facilitative roles, they also used facilitative tag questions frequently. Conversely, women who were not playing facilitative roles did not use facilitative tags frequently.

But if the decisive factor is conversational role rather than gender, how do we explain Janet Holmes's findings, which did show a gender difference? The answer could be that there are simply more contexts in which women take responsibility for facilitating talk. This might, as Holmes suggests, reflect women's preferences about how to conduct a conversation; but it might also reflect social expectations and arrangements which oblige women to do more facilitating whether they like it or not.

One study of heterosexual couples' talk, carried out by the sociologist Pamela Fishman, found that women asked men far more questions (of all kinds, not just tag questions) than men asked women.[8] Questions are often used as opening moves in a conversation: rather than being straightforward requests for information, questions like 'how was your day?' or 'who was at the party?' are invitations to talk about a certain topic. One reason why the women in Fishman's study asked so many questions was that their partners often 'passed' on several proposed topics (by not responding, or responding very minimally) before the women finally came up with something they were interested in discussing.

Fishman's study pre-dates the myth of Mars and Venus, and her explanation was not that women always want to talk whereas men sometimes just want, in John Gray's phrase, to go into their caves. Her data suggested that in many cases the men were not unwilling to converse: once women had offered them a topic they were interested in, they often did most of the talking. But they did not regard it as their responsibility to initiate conversation or find something to talk about. They left it to their female partners to do what Fishman called the 'interactional shitwork'—or less emotively, the work of facilitating talk.

What studies like O'Leary's and Fishman's illustrate is that language-use may be linked to gender in an indirect way. Rather than speaking differently simply because they are women or men, women and men may differ in their patterns of language-use because they are engaged in different activities or are playing different conversational roles. Really, the language-use is linked to the activity or the role: it becomes indirectly linked to gender because of the fact that certain activities and roles are performed more often by men than women, or vice versa. But if you study situations where men and women are doing the same things and playing the same roles, you may find—as Kathy O'Leary did—that the expected differences between men and women do not appear.

What difference does it make if the link between language and gender is direct or indirect? Isn't it just splitting hairs to say: 'well, overall women do use more questions than men, but that's not because they're women, it's because there's a tendency for women to play facilitative roles more than men'? Actually, it makes a lot of difference. If the link between language-use and gender is not direct, but is produced by intervening variables like the activity people are engaged in, the role they are playing, and their status relative to other participants, it means we cannot make the move which is so popular with Mars and Venus experts, from observing a difference in the behaviour of men and women to inferring a 'deeper' difference in their verbal abilities or their rules for conversing.

For instance, what if we find that the male TV presenter and the male doctor in Kathy O'Leary's study go home at the end of the day and behave like the men in Pamela Fishman's research, letting their wives do most of the conversational support work? We can hardly explain this by saying that because they are men they do not know how to facilitate talk. In their professional lives these men are highly skilled facilitators. A more plausible explanation for the way they behave is that language-use is influenced by the roles, relationships, expectations, and obligations that are operative in a particular context. Although we remain men and women in every context, our roles *as* men and women vary from one situation to another, and our linguistic behaviour reflects that variation.

But the complexity of the relationship between language and gender does not stop there. Sometimes, the gender differences which matter most are not differences between women and men, but differences between women and women or men and men.

✴ Acts of identity

In 2006, a British reality TV show called *Ladette to Lady* took a group of 'ladettes' (young working-class women whose lifestyles revolved around going out, getting drunk, behaving in a rowdy way in public, and having casual sex with men) and sent them to an old-fashioned finishing school to be taught how to behave like upper-class 'ladies'. They learnt to bake sponge cakes and arrange flowers; they walked around with books on their heads to teach them deportment. They were also expected to master a particular way of speaking.

One thing their teachers disapproved of was the ladettes' working-class accents, which were dealt with (to no very noticeable effect) by subjecting them to elocution lessons. But speaking like a lady was not just a matter of pronunciation. The ladettes were informed that they talked too much, too loudly, and too explicitly: their language was crude and their manner when addressing others was insufficiently deferential. In mixed company they flirted, joked, and laughed too much, and often conversed on 'unsuitable' subjects. If they wanted to become ladies, these habits had to be unlearned.

Ladette to Lady dramatized the point that there is no such thing as a generic woman, and therefore no such thing as a generic women's way of talking. A ladette's way of talking may be different from a lad's, but it is also different—in many ways, far more different—from a lady's. From the finishing school teachers' perspective, the ladettes were not 'proper' women: their behaviour was coarse and 'unfeminine'. But the ladettes themselves perceived things differently. They saw their own version of femininity as ordinary, and the finishing school version as artificial and stuck-up. This clash of views was most apparent when the teachers got together each week to discuss their pupils' progress, and then expelled the pupil they judged least promising. Interviewed afterwards, the rejected ladettes were often more relieved than disappointed; some were openly critical of the 'ladylike' behaviour they had been made to adopt.

The contrast between the ladettes and the ladies demonstrates that femininity and masculinity come in more than one variety. What it means to be a man or a woman—and therefore what it means to talk like one—is always affected by the other attributes that define a person: their age, class, ethnicity, nationality, education, occupation, sexuality, politics, religious and subcultural allegiances. The significance of these factors for the way people communicate is partly to do with their effect on the activities, roles, and relationships I have already mentioned as important influences on language-use. One reason why ladettes and ladies do not talk in the same way is that they do not on the whole do the same things. But it is also about something less tangible: *identity*.

It is a truism that speaking is an 'act of identity'. Whatever else we may be communicating when we speak, we are always communicating information about who we are. Gender, as one important aspect of identity, is among the things our speech sends messages about. But because gender interacts with other aspects of identity, those messages are never reducible to just 'I am a man, not a woman' or 'I am a woman, not a man'.

An act of identity is also an act of differentiation: conveying to others what sort of person you are means making clear not only who you see yourself as being like, but also who you define yourself as different from. Often, the differences we choose to emphasize in our presentation of ourselves as men and women are not those that distinguish us from the 'opposite' sex so much as those that make us stand out from other members of our own. A ladette's behaviour says: 'I am a woman, but not a "lady" or a "good girl" or a "girly girl" '. An adolescent girl's behaviour may say: 'I am a woman, but I'm not like my mother.' Some straight men act hyper-masculine to put as much distance as possible between themselves and gay men—while some gay men, ironically, adopt a similarly masculine style to distance themselves from other gay men whose style is flamboyantly camp.

As these examples suggest, identity is a local, even parochial concern: it is often the smallest differences that carry the most symbolic weight. These small but significant differences are expressed in all kinds of ways: through the way we dress, our preferred leisure activities and habits of consumption, and, not least, the language we use. Language, with its impressive ability to convey subtle nuances and fine distinctions, is particularly well suited to serve the purpose of distinguishing our own tribe from other tribes, and our own selves from other selves.

This has two implications for our understanding of the relationship between language and gender. First, it means that there will be a relationship. For as long as people consider their gender to be a fundamental part of their identity, the distinction between being a man and being a woman is likely to be marked in some way in their speech. Second, though, it means that there will never be just *one* way of marking the distinction. Different kinds of men and women will do it differently, because their allegiance is not to the global categories 'men' and 'women', it is to particular and much more local forms of masculinity and femininity. For that reason if for no other, it will always be futile to look for one way of speaking that is shared by all women and another quite different way of speaking that is shared by all men.

Yet the myth of Mars and Venus persists in searching for generalizations which encapsulate the essence of all men, of all women, and of the One Big Difference between them. Each writer has his or her own version, but the formula is always the same: 'men do this and women do that'. Deborah Tannen tells us that men talk to gain status, women to make connections;[9] Simon Baron-Cohen proposes that female brains are wired for empathy and male brains for understanding and building complex systems.[10] The jacket blurb on a book entitled *Why Men Don't Iron* announces that men act and women communicate.[11]

These generalizations present a range of problems, but one problem they all have in common is that they treat 'men' and 'women' as internally undifferentiated categories. Regardless of its substance, any claim about men and women that ignores the existence of differences within each group is bound to oversimplify the picture, because it is taking a telescope to something that needs to be examined with a microscope.

✭ Acts of exclusion

Here you might be thinking: 'OK, but aren't there always exceptions to every generalization?' When we are dealing with the social world as opposed to the laws of the physical universe, the short answer to that question is 'yes'. Few generalizations are 100 per cent true. But we still need to be careful about what we describe—or dismiss—as an 'exception'.

In Chapter 1 we saw that many familiar generalizations about the way men and women use language are at odds with the patterns found in non-western societies. Those generalizations do not appear to apply equally to all men and women in modern western societies either. It is evident, for instance, that the young working-class women who featured in *Ladette to Lady* did not fit the picture of women being cooperative, empathetic, indirect, and polite. But are they really 'exceptions', or do they only seem exceptional because the research that has shaped our understanding of what is 'normal' is partial in both senses of the word?

Language and gender research, in common with many other kinds of social research, has had a bias towards studying white western middle-class speakers. Robin Lakoff, for instance, though she did not have research subjects as such, makes clear that her description of women's language was based on her experience of observing men and women in her own social milieu. Other linguists have gathered data by recording conversations among their relatives, friends, and acquaintances. Psychologists, whose experiments may require a large number of subjects, have often used samples composed entirely of college students—the easiest group for university-based researchers to recruit, but also one in which certain kinds of people (like older ones and poorer ones) are under-represented.

In most cases these sampling biases are not the result of any deliberate policy, but have more to do with the fact that most researchers are themselves white middle-class westerners, working in settings where white middle-class speakers are the most readily available research subjects. But the result is that without necessarily meaning or wanting to, researchers end up creating more and more knowledge about the same small group of people. The few studies which deal with other groups, and find their behaviour to be different, are then seen as exceptional cases. We forget that the white middle-class speakers whose behaviour we know so much about do not represent the global norm.

Of course, this does not mean white middle-class speakers are unworthy of being studied. They are neither more nor less interesting than anyone else. The problem arises when statements made specifically about them are treated as if they were statements about men and women in general. Even if researchers themselves make the appropriate disclaimers, in the absence of enough research on other groups there is an ever-present temptation to generalize, extrapolating what is true of *some* men and women to the entire population of men and women.

This tendency is strong in popular Mars and Venus books. Research is often cited to lend academic credibility to a writer's claims, but it is rare for the author to reproduce any of the caveats which appear in the original source or go into detail about how the research was done. The resulting accounts may be more readable than a research paper, but they magnify the distortions already present in the academic literature. They obey what is jokingly said to be the first law of journalism: 'first simplify and then exaggerate'.

Since the mid-1990s, a new wave of language and gender research has set out to fill some of the gaps in our knowledge, and correct some of its most obvious biases. This recent research confirms that many common generalizations about the way men and women communicate are at best only partial truths. The more we expand the range of men and women we study and the range of contexts in which we study them, the more difficult it becomes to maintain the belief that men use language in one way while women use it in another.

That general belief is the foundation of the myth of Mars and Venus. In the chapters that follow I will turn to some of the more specific beliefs that make up the larger edifice.

4

Worlds Apart?
Mars and Venus in Childhood
and Adolescence

An adolescent boy once explained to a researcher how boys were different from girls. 'Guys, I don't think we talk about that much,' he said. 'I think girls talk about, you know, every little relationship, every little thing that's ever happened.'[1]

The myth of Mars and Venus elaborates on this observation. It says that women talk more than men, because they use talk to create intimacy and make connections with other people. Men use talk to accomplish practical goals: they do not feel the need to 'talk about every little thing that's ever happened'. Men do, however, feel more need than women to establish their status in relation to their peers. Whereas women's talk is cooperative and supportive, men's is overtly adversarial and competitive.

In *You Just Don't Understand*, Deborah Tannen proposes that these differences have their origins in childhood play. 'Even if they grow up in the same neighborhood, on the same block, or in the same house,' Tannen says, 'girls and boys grow up in different worlds':[2]

> Boys tend to play outside, in large groups that are hierarchically structured. Their groups have a leader who tells others what to do and how to do it, and resists doing what other boys propose. . . . Boys' games have winners and losers and elaborate systems of rules that are frequently the subject of arguments. Finally, boys are frequently heard to boast of their skill and argue about who is best at what.
>
> Girls, on the other hand, play in small groups or in pairs; the center of a girl's social life is a best friend. . . . In their most frequent games, such as jump rope and hopscotch, everyone gets a turn. Many of their activities (such as playing house) do not have winners and losers. . . . Girls don't give orders; they express their preferences as suggestions . . . They don't grab center stage—they don't want it—so they don't challenge each other directly. And much of the time, they simply sit together and talk. Girls are not accustomed to jockey for status in an obvious way; they are more concerned that they be liked.

Tannen's argument is that the differing activities and social norms of girls' and boys' peer groups teach girls and boys different rules for talking. This, she claims, is the source of the misunderstandings which plague adult male–female relationships. Childhood separation makes the two sexes as different in their ways of communicating as people of different nationalities or ethnicities. 'Conversation between men and women is cross-cultural communication.'[3]

The question of male–female misunderstanding is one I return to in Chapter 5. Here I want to look at the question of gender differences in the talk of children and adolescents. Is it true that girls and women talk about 'every little thing', while 'guys don't talk about that much'? Is girls' talk cooperative and boys' talk competitive? And if these differences do exist, is Tannen right about the reasons for them?

✴ Competition and cooperation

Below are two extracts from real conversations recorded by the researcher Judith Baxter.[4] The speakers, 14–15-year-old school pupils, have been told to imagine that they are survivors of a plane crash in the desert, equipped with various items scavenged from the wreckage (such as sunglasses, a compass, and a first aid kit). Their task is to rank the items in order of importance for survival. They are working, by their own choice, in single-sex groups: one of the extracts below comes from a discussion among boys, while the other is from an all-girls' group. Is it possible to guess which is which by analysing how competitively or cooperatively the two groups talk?

Group A

S: wouldn't you need the sunglasses?

C: yeah, that's what I think

S: because it would be really hot and protect yourself from the sun and you'd be able to see more

G: yeah, but if you're trying to live, does it matter [whether you can see?

C: [you can go *blind*

G: exactly, but if you're trying to survive, does it really matter?

C: (sounding irritated) I wouldn't [want to go *blind*

S: [it does, because if you were blind you wouldn't be able to see what you were doing and you would end up dying anyway.
You'd have less chance of surviving anyway.

G: yeah, but you're not likely to go blind unless you're looking right up into the sun

Group B

C: (pointing) right, what did you put?

M: compass.

C: (pointing) what did you put?

T: I put sunglasses

C: right, I put the parachute (gives long explanation for choosing it)

Other voices: mirror, mirror . . . the torch

C: and you could use a gun, couldn't you? You could shoot—

H: you could shoot the pilot

C: right. So has anyone changed their mind? (pointing) What do you think?

H: I say compass

T: I think sunglasses are quite important because you have to be able to see what it says on the compass for a start (laughter from the group)

H: you could just go like that (mimes shading eyes) shut your eyes for a moment

C: right. You go (pointing) Say why you thought the first aid kit.

It could be argued that Group B's interaction is more cooperative. Although there is a dominant speaker—C, who acts as the unofficial chairperson, nominating people to speak and generally directing the discussion—four out of C's six turns are used to facilitate discussion by eliciting opinions from others. Another cooperative feature of this exchange is the absence or avoidance of overt conflict: where group-members disagree (as T and H do about the relative merits of the sunglasses and the compass), they do so politely, using mitigating strategies like hedging ('I *think* sunglasses are *quite* important') and humour.

In Group A's discussion, by contrast, there is more evidence of competition. The extract begins cooperatively: the first three turns are used by S and C to develop a consensus in favour of the sunglasses. But conflict develops as G repeatedly challenges the others. The resulting exchange has a distinctly uncooperative flavour. The participants interrupt each other, show signs of becoming irritated, and do not seem to be moving towards any conclusion. All this might lead us to guess that Group A is the boys' group and Group B the girls' group.

But it would also be possible to argue the opposite case. For instance, it could be observed that Group B's discussion is more structured and businesslike, largely because they accept being told what to do by C. Although C adopts a facilitative role, the style is notably brisk, using direct questions ('right, what did you put?') and imperatives ('Say why you thought the first aid kit'). In Group A, no one takes charge in the same way. Perhaps, then, Group A are the girls and group B the boys.

In fact, Group A *are* the girls and Group B the boys. But if you do not already know which group is which, it is difficult to deduce it from linguistic evidence alone. Each group's conversation contains both 'competitive' and 'cooperative' elements; some of the strategies used could be given either a 'competitive' or a 'cooperative' interpretation. For instance, C in group B could be described either as 'facilitating talk' (a cooperative and often female role) or as 'telling others what to do and how to do it' (an assertion of leadership which Tannen associates with boys' behaviour in hierarchically structured groups). Once you know C is a boy, though, it is tempting to use that information to resolve the ambiguity—in other words, to interpret his behaviour as on balance more 'directive' than 'facilitative'. The claim that boys' talk is more competitive can thus become a self-fulfilling prophecy.

★ Different for girls?

We might, though, have more difficulty interpreting the behaviour of S[ophie], C[harlotte], and G[ina], the girls in

Group A, as 'cooperative and supportive'. Their interaction is difficult to reconcile with Tannen's observation that girls 'don't challenge each other directly' and are not interested in 'jockeying for status', but are 'more concerned that they be liked'. Gina makes three overt challenges to Sophie and Charlotte, persisting despite the signs that they think she is being obnoxious. She does not seem overly concerned about whether Sophie and Charlotte like her. So what exactly is going on here?

After the group sessions, Judith Baxter interviewed the pupils involved and their class teacher about what they thought had been going on. By chance, Sophie was absent when the girls were interviewed. The others (including a girl named Helen, who was present in the discussion but did not contribute to the extract I reproduced from it) took the opportunity to complain about Sophie's behaviour:[5]

Charlotte: I didn't agree with anything Sophie was saying. She wanted to be the leader. To be in charge. I felt a bit uncomfortable with that.

Gina and Helen: Yes, so did I

This might seem surprising, since in the extract we have looked at it is clear that Charlotte aligns herself with Sophie against Gina. But the girls' teacher also commented to Baxter that the group had resisted Sophie's leadership. 'You could see resentment bubbling up . . . they interrupted and challenged her for the sake of it.'[6] This 'bitchiness' was said by the girls to be a disadvantage of working in all-female groups. Asked how they thought mixed groups were different, Helen replied: 'Boys aren't as bitchy as girls. And girls aren't as bitchy towards blokes.'[7]

Judith Baxter is one of a number of researchers who have pointed out that girls' preoccupation with 'being liked' is not the *opposite* of boys' concern with status, it is a version of the same thing. Being liked—also known as 'popularity'—is an important form of status for children of both sexes (ask any parent of an unpopular child), and it has consequences for their linguistic behaviour. Baxter has found that the dominant speakers in the classroom are usually those who are popular outside the classroom. Popular pupils, like Sophie in the girls' group and Charlie in the boys' group, are able to gain a disproportionate share of the speaking time, and to command respect for what they say, because of the active support and approval of their peers. Less popular pupils like Gina have to fight harder to gain the floor, and what they say is often resisted.

But there does seem to be a difference between boys like Charlie and girls like Sophie. Popular girls tend to attract resentment from their peers when they try to assume leadership roles, whereas this is not so true for popular boys. Baxter's interview with the boys did not elicit any complaints about Charlie's behaviour. When she asked the class teacher about it, the teacher replied: 'They all responded to it. They felt fine that he had adopted this role.'[8]

Baxter suggests that this difference arises because girls themselves subscribe to the view that overtly dominant behaviour is less acceptable for females than for males. Girls 'aren't as bitchy towards blokes' who behave like Sophie because male leadership is acceptable to both sexes. By contrast, a popular girl who flaunts her status in a way that is seen as transgressing the norms of femininity will be punished for it. That is the reason why girls often go about things in a more covert way—for instance by criticizing others behind their backs and spreading rumours about them. Girls are no less competitive than boys (and their peer groups are no less hierarchical); but the ideological opposition between femininity and power gives them less freedom to 'jockey for status in an obvious way'.

Some researchers have challenged the belief that girls generally rely on indirect strategies for establishing status hierarchies. In her book *The Hidden Life of Girls*, based on more than 100 hours of video and audio recordings of a group of six 9–12-year-old girls who were studied over a period of three years, the ethnographer Marjorie Harness Goodwin describes a side of girls' social life that she believes has been downplayed in previous research because it does not fit with the expectation that boys will be assertive while girls are supportive and nurturing.[9]

The girls in Goodwin's study—a socially and ethnically mixed group attending a progressive private school in Los Angeles—habitually did all the things which Tannen says girls do not do. They gave direct orders, challenged one another directly, argued about the rules of hopscotch, and boasted about their athletic skills, possessions, and family status. They also engaged in bullying a 'tag-along girl'—their term for a child who wanted to join their clique but who was never accepted as a legitimate member. Their bullying did not only take the forms stereotypically associated with girls, such as spreading rumours about the 'tag-along' or refusing to play with her. It also involved direct confrontation and verbal abuse.

Not all the confrontational behaviour Goodwin observed was directed at other girls, however. In the following extract from her data, the girls are organizing a soccer game when a group of boys arrives and demands possession of the field.[10]

Emi: We have it today

Ron: We play soccer every day, OK?

Miguel: It's more boys than girls

Emi: *So*? Your point?

Ron: This is *our* field

Emi: It's not your field. Did you pay for it? No. Your name is not written on this land.

Kathy: Mine is. (writing in the dirt) K-A-T-H-Y!

Goodwin points out that the girls' behaviour during this exchange is at odds with the Mars and Venus view that girls try to avoid open conflict by expressing themselves in indirect and polite language. Emi's stance could hardly be more confrontational: she begins with a bald assertion that the girls are in possession of the field ('We have it today.'), goes on to challenge the relevance of what Ron and Miguel say in response ('*So*? Your point?'), and then directly contradicts Ron's statement that the field is a boys' space ('It's not your field'). Neither she nor Kathy makes any concession to the boys: they do not apologize, hedge, or try to negotiate a compromise. Their language is as direct and as forceful as that of their opponents.

✭ Market forces

Deborah Tannen emphasizes that gender differences emerge very early, and then persist, because of the near-total separation between boys' and girls' peer groups. Goodwin's research illustrates that the social worlds of boys and girls are not completely isolated from one another. However, their relationship changes over time. The exchange Goodwin witnessed on the soccer field took place when the girls were in fifth grade. Some research has suggested that this is often a turning point.

The linguist Penelope Eckert spent several years studying a group of girls in northern California as they moved through elementary school and into junior high school. She observed a significant change in the behaviour of boys and girls—but especially girls—between the fifth and sixth grades:[11]

> It is not uncommon in fifth grade to see girls and boys running around, making sudden movements, rolling on the floor or throwing themselves to the ground, using their bodies in much the same way. Increasingly in sixth grade, girls stop running and

start monitoring their facial expressions, striking feminine and dramatic poses, adorning and inspecting their hands in a disembodied manner, arranging their breasts. And boys begin to subdue their facial expressions, control their hair, spread out their shoulders, develop deliberate tough or athletic walks and flamboyant moves on the athletic field or court, consciously deepen their voices. . . . As boys take over casual playground sports, girls replace vigorous physical playground activity with observing, heckling, and occasionally disrupting boys' games, and with sitting or walking around in small and large groups.

What is happening to these boys and girls is that they are beginning to participate in an emerging 'heterosexual market'. Although they are still pre-adolescent, and in most cases not yet interested in sex as such, their interest in the trappings of adult heterosexuality is driven by what Eckert points out is an overriding social imperative among children: the need to demonstrate maturity by moving away from the 'babyish' behaviour of the past. For pre-adolescents, this entails cultivating more 'adult' forms of masculinity and femininity that obey the heterosexual principle 'opposites attract'.

Though both sexes are engaged in this project, it changes the girls' lives more profoundly. Boys cultivate a more adult masculinity through the same activities that were important to them before—for instance, sporting activities that show off their physical strength and athletic skill. For girls, on the other hand, cultivating a more adult femininity means replacing the activities and accomplishments of childhood with a different set of preoccupations. In particular, they abandon physical play: instead of using their bodies to do things, they start to focus on grooming and adorning them. They watch boys' games from the sidelines, or as Tannen notes, 'simply sit together and talk'.

The move from doing to talking is recognized by girls as a significant rite of passage. Halfway through fifth grade, two of the girls Eckert was studying, Trudy and Katya, took her aside and told her excitedly that instead of playing jump-rope at recess as they had always done before, they now spent some recess periods 'just talking'. In case Eckert had missed the significance of this, they spelled it out for her: these grown-up conversations were all about *boys*.

The girls talk more about boys than boys talk about them. In fact, the main function of 'going with' a boy, for girls of this age, is to give you something to talk about with your girl-friends; the heterosexual relationships themselves are usually brief and perfunctory. But through their intense discussions of these insubstantial liaisons, girls are learning a new language of relationships and feelings, and making this area of experience their own. They are also establishing new hierarchies among themselves. By attracting boys' interest and appearing at ease with the world of 'mature' romantic relationships, a girl gains status among her female peers.

Eckert suggests that the girls' behaviour is a response to being marginalized in activities which were previously open to both sexes. 'Seeing that they won't gain recognition for the pursuits that boys are taking over, girls choose to call the shots, and to become experts, in a whole new arena.'[12]

Although this choice is precipitated by the increasing inequality between boys and girls as they move towards adolescence, girls like Trudy, who are successful players in the market, experience it as a source of excitement and power.

⭐ Separate cultures or separate spheres?

Eckert's research supports the idea that shared activity is more important to boys whereas talking is more important to girls. It also confirms (as does Goodwin's work) that girls are more intensely engaged in talking about people, relationships, and feelings. But there are nevertheless significant differences between Eckert's account and Tannen's. Tannen says that boys and girls are different because they grow up from the first in separate social worlds; Eckert complicates this with her observation that the differences between boys and girls become sharper at precisely the moment when their social worlds are becoming *less* separate, because the growing importance of heterosexual attraction brings them into more direct contact.

This difference reflects a deeper difference in theoretical approach. Tannen adopts what she calls a 'cross-cultural approach', in which male and female peer groups are likened to different cultures. On this view, misunderstandings between the sexes are like the problems that can arise when Americans try to do business in Japan, or when Italians attempt to make conversation with Finns. The underlying problem is simply unfamiliarity with the other's way of doing things.

But how convincing is the cultural analogy? The differences between Finnish and Italian communication norms clearly do arise from cultural separation. Finns do not grow up explicitly comparing themselves to Italians or consciously trying to distinguish themselves from Italians. For the average Finn, the behaviour of Italians is both unfamiliar and irrelevant. But the same surely cannot be said of males and females in one culture. Masculinity and femininity are defined in opposition to one other, and the significance of gender distinctions is something children become aware of at an early age. Nor is it a random matter which qualities and behaviours are defined as 'masculine' and which are defined as 'feminine'. The qualities and behaviours considered appropriate for each sex are related to the place each is destined to occupy in the world.

Perhaps the 'separation' which is relevant here is not so much the childhood separation between boys' and girls' peer groups as the traditional separation between the male-dominated public sphere and the female-dominated private sphere. Penelope Eckert argues that 'the origins of gender differences in styles of interaction can be traced to the traditional roles that relegate women to the domestic realm and men to the economic marketplace'. Though these roles have changed to some extent, 'the norms of interaction that have come to be associated with them remain to complicate and thwart social change'.[13] Her pre-adolescent girl subjects illustrate her point: they have grasped the reality of male dominance in public arenas, and are preparing themselves instead to take leading roles in the private domain of intimate relationships.

Yet that does not mean they are unconcerned about power and status. The social world Trudy and her sixth-grade peers are busy creating is full of competition and conflict (just like the world of the slightly younger girls studied by Marjorie Goodwin), but its focus has shifted to reflect their new pre-occupations. Instead of fighting with boys, the girls now fight over boys; instead of accusing other girls of trying to cheat at hopscotch, they accuse them of trying to steal their boyfriends.

✴ 'Guys don't talk about that much ...'

What about the idea that boys and men do not make connections with each other through talk about people, their behaviour, and their relationships? In 1990, a male student in one of my classes recorded a conversation among the men he shared a house with. The student wanted to investigate what male friends talk about, and he reported that his friends favoured stereotypically male topics: sport, drinking, and sex with women, all of which tended to be discussed in a 'competitive' way that put the speaker's own prowess in the foreground.

But when I read his transcript, I noticed a topic which he had not commented on, despite the fact that it took up more time than any other except for sport. That topic was other men: men the speakers disapproved of because, allegedly, they were gay. The following extract comes from a longer sequence in which the men discuss a series of supposedly gay classmates.[14]

Bryan: uh you know that really gay guy in our Age of Revolution class who sits in front of us? he wore shorts again, by the way, it's like 42 degrees out he wore shorts again [laughter] it's like a speedo, he wears a speedo to class he's got incredibly skinny legs you know

Ed: you know like those shorts women volleyball players wear? it's like those it's like French cut spandex

Bryan: you know what's even more ridiculous? When you wear those shorts and like a parka on

Bryan: he's either got some condition that he's got to like have his legs exposed at all times or else he's got really good legs

Ed: he's probably he's he's like he's like at home combing his leg hairs

Carl: he really likes his legs

Bryan: he doesn't have any leg hair though

Ed: he *really* likes his legs

Al: very long very white and very skinny

Bryan: yes and oh those ridiculous Reeboks that are always (indecipherable) and goofy white socks always striped tube socks

Ed: he's the antithesis of man

The obvious description of what these male friends are doing is 'gossiping': talking about other people in a critical or disapproving way. Sociologists and anthropologists who have studied gossip say that it usually serves two main purposes.

First, it is an unofficial conduit for information—a valuable commodity in most communities. Second, it reinforces the bonds between participants, and affirms their worth, by contrasting them with the absent others whose social or moral transgressions are being gossiped about.

The extract above seems to have both functions. The men are exchanging information about others' private lives which is not available through more 'official' channels (on this campus in 1990, it was rare for gay and lesbian students to make their sexual preferences public). In addition, though, their criticisms of the 'really gay guy' allow these straight men to bond around their common understanding of what masculinity is and what it is not. They are 'real men', whereas the target of their gossip is, in Ed's phrase, 'the antithesis of man'.

Evidently gossip is not just for girls. In fact, studies generally find that both sexes engage in it. Robin Dunbar, an evolutionary scientist who we will meet again in Chapter 6, found that in the sample of people he studied, 'exchanging social information'—his broad definition of gossip—accounted for about 70 per cent of talk among both men and women.[15] So why does gossip have such strong (and negative) associations with women?

The answer may have something to do with the use women have traditionally made of gossip as a covert means of gaining power. The historical linguists Terttu Nevalainen and Helena Raumolin-Brunberg, who have examined evidence relating to men's and women's use of language in Tudor and Stuart England, point out that in the overwhelmingly male dominated society of the time, gossip was one of the few weapons women had at their disposal.[16] The potential of women's gossip to ruin a man's reputation, deservedly or otherwise, was both acknowledged and feared by men, who were quick to denounce gossip as a peculiarly vicious female habit.

Girls like the ones studied by Judith Baxter, Marjorie Goodwin, and Penelope Eckert continue to use gossip as a weapon, though mainly against each other. This too attracts negative judgements, along the lines of 'boys fight fair, girls are devious backstabbers'. But such criticisms overlook both the reasons why girls and women use gossip in the ways they do, and the fact that boys and men also gossip.

⭐ Dominance and difference: a false opposition?

When Deborah Tannen wrote *You Just Don't Understand*, the best-known approach to gender differences in language was still the one pioneered by Robin Lakoff in the early 1970s, which treated the differences primarily as effects of male dominance and female subordination. Tannen wanted to avoid what she saw as the pitfalls of this 'dominance' approach: either blaming men for oppressing women, or blaming women for lacking assertiveness. 'Taking a cross-cultural approach', she says, 'makes it possible to explain why dissatisfactions are justified without accusing anyone of being wrong or crazy.'[17]

But by trying to divorce gender entirely from power, the cross-cultural approach threw the baby out with the bathwater. There is a world of difference between the view Tannen attributes to 'dominance' theorists—that individual men talking to individual women consciously and deliberately set out to dominate them—and the argument advanced by researchers like Baxter, Goodwin, and Eckert, that both sexes' behaviour is influenced by the power structures of the wider society. The first claim is untenable, at least as a general proposition; but the second is crucial for our understanding of the relationship between language and gender.

It might seem that patterns of interaction in single-sex peer groups cannot, by definition, have anything to do with inequality between the sexes. How can boys dominate girls when there are no girls there to be dominated? When you observe girls talking to girls and boys talking to boys, it is tempting to think that you are observing femininity and masculinity in their purest forms. But this is a naive assumption. Children's single-sex peer groups do not exist in a social vacuum, and gender inequalities in the wider society do not only show up in direct acts of domination by males over females. They also affect the way the two sexes behave among themselves. Inequality is the reason why girls and boys often compete for different kinds of status, and why girls often assert power in more 'devious' ways than boys.

The contrast between 'dominance' and 'difference' is a false opposition: gender as a social system is about both simultaneously. Though recent research does support the claim that male and female peer group cultures are different in certain ways, it also suggests that inequalities of power influence the form the differences take. Saying that boys and men talk to gain status while girls and women talk to make connections, or that male talk is competitive and female talk is cooperative, both oversimplifies the realities of linguistic behaviour and fails to explain the reasons why certain gender-related tendencies exist.

But the claims the cross-cultural approach makes about communication in male and female peer groups are only half the story. The other half is about what happens when Mars and Venus collide. In the next chapter, we will look in more detail at the now-widespread belief that when men and women talk to each other, they often 'just don't understand'.

5

Cross-purposes:
The Myth of Male–Female
Misunderstanding

John Gray's *Men Are from Mars, Women Are from Venus* contains
a chapter entitled 'Speaking Different Languages'.[1] In it Gray
says that the 'original' Martians and Venusians communicated
without difficulty, because they knew their languages were
mutually incomprehensible. Modern men and women, by
contrast, are under the illusion that they speak the same
language. But though the words they use may be the same,
their meanings for each sex are different. The result is that
men and women often do not understand one another.

The idea that men and women metaphorically 'speak
different languages' is not, of course, new, but the myth of
Mars and Venus has given it new currency and legitimacy.
What was once just a metaphor has acquired the status
of literal, scientific truth. Today it is widely believed that
misunderstanding between men and women is a widespread
and serious problem. But is our concern about it justified

by the evidence, or is 'male–female miscommunication' a myth?

✸ Crosstalk

The most influential popular account of male–female miscommunication—Deborah Tannen's in *You Just Don't Understand* —does have roots in linguistic research, but not research on language and gender. As a student, Tannen worked with John Gumperz, a specialist in the study of communication between people of different ethnic groups. Gumperz showed that subtle differences in the way two ethnic groups used language could lead to what he called 'crosstalk': systematic misunderstandings which neither group was conscious of.[2]

One case of crosstalk studied by Gumperz occurred between white and South Asian (Indian or Pakistani) speakers of English at Heathrow Airport in London. White workers who used the staff cafeteria were irritated by Asian servers' habit of offering them gravy on their food while saying the word 'gravy' with a falling intonation. In non-Asian British English it is more usual to signal an offer by using rising intonation, as if asking a question: '[do you want] gravy?' To the white workers, the Asians sounded as if they were either unnecessarily stating 'this is gravy', or worse, telling them they were going to get gravy on their food whether they wanted it or not.

But on investigation it became clear that these meanings were not what the Asian workers intended. When Gumperz played recordings of the utterance 'gravy', spoken with falling intonation, to samples of white and Asian speakers, and asked them what they thought it meant, there was a difference in the answers they gave. White speakers said it meant 'this is gravy'—a bald statement of fact—whereas Asian speakers said it meant 'would you like some gravy?'—a polite offer. The two groups were operating with different systems for using intonation to signal whether an utterance was intended as a statement or a question. But because they were not aware of this difference, each group was misinterpreting the other's intentions. The white workers thought the Asians were rude; the Asians thought the white workers were racist.

Deborah Tannen took the idea of crosstalk from research on interethnic communication and applied it to the case of male–female communication. She was not the only scholar to do so. In 1982, Daniel Maltz and Ruth Borker published an article in a book edited by Gumperz (Tannen was another contributor) which explored the possibility that gender differences might function like ethnic differences.[3] To illustrate how the analogy might work, they cited a gender difference that had been reported in a number of studies: the finding that women used more minimal responses—brief acknowledgements of others' speech like 'yeah', 'uh huh', and 'mm'—than men did.

Just as certain intonation patterns had turned out in Gumperz's research to have different meanings for white and Asian speakers, Maltz and Borker speculated that minimal responses might turn out to have different meanings for men and women. Perhaps women used them to mean 'yes, I'm listening to you', whereas men used them to mean 'yes, I agree with you'. If that were so, it would provide a simple explanation of why women use minimal responses more frequently than men: conversationalists generally do more listening than agreeing. It might also suggest a crosstalk interpretation of the common female complaint that men do not listen. If women think minimal responses mean 'I'm listening', they are likely to take the absence of minimal responses as evidence that men are not listening. But if men use minimal responses to signal agreement rather than listening, then the women are mistaken: their irritation is based on a misunderstanding.

But for this crosstalk argument to work, we have to accept not only that men and women use the same linguistic form differently, but also that they are as unfamiliar with one another's ways of using it as the white and Asian speakers Gumperz studied. On reflection, that is not very plausible. The ethnic groups in Gumperz's research grew up in different countries (the Asians were mostly foreign-born immigrants), spoke different dialects of English (which for many of the Asians was a second language), and had very little contact with each other outside the workplace. Men and women from one community are not a parallel case. Even if they do use some linguistic forms differently, they have enough experience of interacting with each other to make the differences comprehensible.

In any case, there is simply no evidence that minimal responses do mean different things to men and women. Unlike Gumperz in the interethnic case, Maltz and Borker did not carry out systematic tests to see if men and women interpreted the same minimal responses differently. The point of their article was to raise the possibility that a gender difference might exist, and suggest that this should be investigated in future research. But as happens all too frequently with claims about male–female differences, what was put forward as a speculation soon started to be cited as a fact.

One researcher did later test Maltz and Borker's proposal using techniques similar to Gumperz's. Helen Reid-Thomas played recordings of exchanges containing minimal responses to male and female judges, and asked them whether they thought the 'yes' or 'mhm' meant 'I'm listening, go on', 'I agree with you', or something else.[4] If Maltz and Borker were right, Reid-Thomas expected to find a tendency for men to favour the 'I agree' interpretation and for women to lean towards the 'I'm listening' interpretation. But in fact she found no difference. Informants of both sexes took some minimal responses to indicate listening and others to indicate agreement: they also concurred in their judgements of which were which. Reid-Thomas concluded that it is the context which tells people how to interpret minimal responses, and that the gender of the interpreter is irrelevant.

Claims about male–female misunderstanding have proliferated since the 1980s, but many have never been tested in any rigorous way. They are based on speculation, or on purely anecdotal evidence. A case in point is the claim that men favour a direct style of speaking and have difficulty understanding women who prefer to go about things more indirectly. Like Maltz and Borker's speculation about minimal responses, the idea that men find indirectness difficult to understand is not supported by evidence; but it remains a common folk-belief, and in some contexts, as we will see, it can have serious consequences.

★ Speaking directly

Before the myth of Mars and Venus, the idea that women communicate less directly than men was associated with concerns about women's alleged lack of assertiveness and confidence. The importance of speaking directly was a staple topic in assertiveness training, and advice based on the same principle was common in self-help books and women's magazines, especially those addressed to professional women. For instance, an article in *Options* magazine on '10 Classic Career Mistakes All Women Make' lists using 'tentative language' as number 9:[5]

> How many times have you heard someone say things like 'I'm not really sure if I'm right, but perhaps . . .'? With that kind of talk, who is going to believe we are confident in what we are saying? . . . Too often we make statements as if they were questions, such as, 'we'll bring the deadline forward, OK?'

Options counsels women to avoid tentative language on the grounds that it makes them sound weak and indecisive—the argument put forward by Robin Lakoff in her influential 1970s text *Language and Woman's Place*. But over time, a different argument has become more popular. The following tip comes from *Glamour* magazine: 'Speak directly to male subordinates. Women tend to shy away from giving a blatant order, but men find the indirect approach manipulative and confusing.' Here women are told to speak directly to men, not because indirectness undermines their authority, but because men find it 'manipulative and confusing'. The substance of the advice has not changed, but the theory behind it has shifted from a 'deficit model' of gender difference (women's ways of speaking are inferior to men's) to a 'cross-cultural approach' (the two styles are equally valid, but the difference between them can lead to misunderstanding).

This raises two questions. First, if the male and female styles are equally valid, why does it always seem to be women who are told they must accommodate to men's preferences— even, apparently, when the men are their subordinates? Is avoiding male–female miscommunication an exclusively female responsibility? Second, though, why is it assumed that indirectness causes miscommunication in the first place? What is the evidence that men are confused by it?

Glamour is not the only source for this allegation. In a section of *Men Are from Mars, Women Are from Venus* which explains how to ask men to do things, John Gray says that women should avoid using indirect requests. For instance, they should not signal that they would like a man to bring in the shopping by saying 'the groceries are in the car': they should ask him directly, by saying 'would you bring in the groceries?' Another mistake women make is to formulate requests using the word *could* rather than *would*. ' "Could you empty the trash?"', says Gray, 'is merely a question gathering information. "Would you empty the trash?" is a request.'[6]

Gray seems to be suggesting that men hear utterances like 'could you empty the trash?' as purely hypothetical questions about their ability to perform the action mentioned. But that is a patently ridiculous claim. No competent user of English would take 'could you empty the trash?' as 'merely a question gathering information', any more than they would take 'could you run a mile in four minutes?' as a polite request to start running. Gray is right to think that the 'could you do X?' formula has both functions, but wrong to suppose that this causes confusion. Human languages are not codes in which each word or expression has a single, predetermined meaning. Rather, human communication relies on the ability of humans to put the words someone utters together with other information about the world, and on that basis infer what the speaker intended to communicate to them.

Take the case of someone saying 'the groceries are in the car' and meaning 'please bring them into the house'. How do we get from the form to the meaning? The answer is that we do not stop at decoding the statement 'the groceries are in the car', but also mentally ask ourselves: 'Why is she telling me the groceries are in the car? What would make that a relevant thing for her to say at this moment?' We then use our background knowledge—propositions like 'groceries are kept in houses, not cars', and 'if one member of a household has just been shopping, it is reasonable for them to ask for help unloading the shopping'—to infer that the speaker's intention is not merely to inform us of the whereabouts of the groceries, but to ask us to bring them from the car into the house.

Some individuals—for instance, people with autism—may indeed find indirectness confusing; they find a great deal of human communication confusing, because their condition impairs their ability to make inferences about what is going on in other people's minds. But this kind of problem is exceptional: we define it as a disability precisely because the ability to infer others' intentions plays such a crucial role in communication. Does John Gray think that maleness is a disability? And if he really believes that men cannot process indirect requests *from* women, how does he explain the fact that men quite frequently make indirect requests *to* women?

A friend once told me a story about the family dinners of her childhood. Each night as the family sat down to eat, her father would examine the food on his plate and then say to his wife something like: 'is there any ketchup, Vera?' His wife would then get up and fetch whatever condiment he had mentioned. According to John Gray's theory, he should have reacted with surprise: 'oh, I didn't mean I wanted ketchup, I was just asking whether we had any'. Needless to say, that was not his reaction. Both he and his wife understood 'is there any ketchup?' as an indirect request to get the ketchup, rather than 'merely a question gathering information'.

Yet if my friend made the same request, her mother's response was different: she treated it as an information question and said: 'yes, dear, it's in the cupboard'. Presumably, that was not because she had suddenly become incapable of understanding indirectness. Rather, she *pretended* to hear her daughter's request as an information question because she wanted to send her a message along the lines of, 'I may get ketchup for your father, but I don't feel obliged to do the same for you'.

What this example illustrates is that some 'misunderstandings' are tactical rather than real. Pretending not to understand what someone wants you to do is one way to avoid doing it. This may be what is really going on when a man claims not to have recognized a woman's 'could you empty the trash?' or 'the groceries are in the car' as a request. The 'real' conflict is not about what was meant, it is about who is entitled to expect what services from whom.

By recasting this type of domestic dispute as a problem of 'male–female miscommunication', the myth of Mars and Venus just obscures the real issue. And while arguments about who empties the trash or unloads the groceries may be petty, there are other conflicts between men and women where far more is at stake.

★ 'Just say no'

At a Canadian university in the 1990s, two women students made complaints against the same male student after they discovered by chance that they had both, on separate occasions, gone out on a date with him and been sexually assaulted at the end of the evening. Their complaints were heard by a university tribunal whose proceedings were recorded for a linguistic research project.[7]

Like many rape and sexual assault cases, this one turned on whether or not the defendant could reasonably have believed that the complainants consented to sex. Both incidents had begun consensually, with the women inviting the man into their room and engaging in activities such as kissing and touching; but they claimed he had gone on to force them into further sexual activity which they made clear they did not want. He maintained that they did want it—or at least, had said nothing to make him think that they did not.

In this extract from the hearing, one of the complainants, MB, has just told the tribunal that the defendant persisted in touching her even after she had repeatedly communicated to him that she did not want to have sex. A tribunal member, GK, then asks her the following question:

> And did it occur to you through the persistent behaviour that maybe your signals were not coming across loud and clear, that 'I'm not getting through what I want and what I don't want?' . . . This is the whole thing about getting signals mixed up. We all socialize in one way or the other to read signals and to give signals. In that particular context, were you at all concerned your signals were not being read exactly and did you think since signals were not being read correctly for you, 'should I do something different with my signals?'

GK evidently interprets the incident as a case of miscommunication ('getting signals mixed up'). She also appears to hold the complainant responsible for the breakdown in communication. She phrases her initial question using a formula ('did it occur to you that . . . ?') which usually implies that the point *should* have occurred to the addressee. Her subsequent questions ('were you at all concerned that . . . ?' 'did you think that . . . [you] should . . . ?') are phrased in a similarly loaded way. GK is not so much asking about MB's view of events as communicating her own: MB should have realized that her signals were not getting through, and she should have acted on that realization by 'doing something different with [her] signals'.

Susan Ehrlich, the linguist who analysed the tribunal proceedings, notes that the defendant is never challenged in the same way about his response to the complainants' signals. At one point he is asked why he persisted in sexual activity with MB when she was either asleep or pretending to be asleep. He replies: 'she said that she was tired, you know, she never said like "no", "stop", "don't", you know, "don't do this" uhm "get out of bed" '. Nobody asks him why he did not consider the possibility that by saying she was tired and then apparently falling asleep, MB was communicating that she wanted him to stop. You don't have to be a rocket scientist to work out that someone who feigns unconsciousness while in bed with you probably doesn't want to have sex. But nobody criticizes the defendant for being so obtuse. In these proceedings, the assumption does seem to be that avoiding miscommunication is not a shared responsibility, but specifically a female one.

This assumption both reflects and reinforces the traditional tendency of rape trials—especially where the parties are acquainted—to focus more on the character and behaviour of the complainant than on that of the alleged perpetrator. Her

clothing, her alcohol consumption, her previous sexual conduct and reputation, are all scrutinized minutely for any sign
that she might have been willing all along. By suggesting that
men have trouble understanding any refusal which is not max-
imally direct, the myth of Mars and Venus has added to the
burden judicial proceedings place on women who claim to
have been raped. They can now be challenged not only to prove
that they did not consent to sex, but also that they refused in a
manner sufficiently direct to preclude misunderstanding.

The women in the Canadian case were unable to satisfy
the tribunal on that point. The tribunal's written judgement
criticized their behaviour:

> There is little doubt that both complainants did not expressly
> object to some of the activity that took place that evening. It
> is also clear that their actions at times did not unequivocally
> indicate a lack of willing participation.[8]

The defendant was found guilty, but the tribunal declined
to impose the recommended punishment, expulsion from the
university. Instead they banned him from campus dormitory
buildings. This decision reflected their view that the complainants were partly responsible for what had happened to
them. Had they communicated differently, they could have
prevented it.

That idea also features prominently in sex education and
'rape prevention' programmes, which instruct women that if
they do not want to have sex they should 'just say no'. It is
stressed that a woman's refusal should take the form of a firm,

unvarnished 'no' (spoken in a tone and accompanied by body-language that makes clear it is a real rather than a token refusal), and that it is not necessary—in fact it is counter-productive—to give reasons for refusing. Only by keeping the message short and simple can you be sure that it will not be misunderstood. This advice may be well intentioned, but linguistic research suggests it is highly questionable.

The researchers Celia Kitzinger and Hannah Frith conducted focus-group interviews with fifty-eight women and asked them how, in practice, they communicated to men that they did not wish to have sex.[9] Despite being familiar with the standard rape prevention advice, all but a tiny handful of the women told Kitzinger and Frith that they would never 'just say no'. They judged this to be an unacceptable way of doing things, and likely to make matters worse by giving men an additional reason to feel aggrieved.

The strategies the women actually reported using were designed to 'soften the blow', as one put it, in various ways. One popular tactic was to provide a reason for refusing which made reference to a woman's inability, as opposed to her unwillingness, to have sex. Examples included the time-honoured 'I've got a headache', 'I'm really tired', and 'I've got my period'. As one woman explained, such excuses would prevent the man from 'getting really upset' or 'blaming you'. Another softening tactic was to preface the refusal with something like 'I'm incredibly flattered, but . . .'. Women also reported telling men that they were not yet ready for sex when they knew in reality that they would never be interested.

All this might seem like depressing evidence that psychologists are right about women lacking assertiveness, confidence, or self-esteem—except for one crucial fact. All the strategies the women reported using in this situation are also used, by both sexes, in every other situation where it is necessary to verbalize a refusal. Research on conversational patterns shows that in everyday contexts, refusing is never done by 'just saying no'. Most refusals do not even contain the word 'no'. Yet in non-sexual situations, no one seems to have trouble understanding them.

If this sounds counter-intuitive, let us consider a concrete example. Suppose a colleague says to me casually as I pass her in the corridor: 'a few of us are going to the pub after work, do you want to come?' This is an invitation, which calls for me to respond with either an acceptance or a refusal. If I am going to accept, I can simply say 'yes, I'd love to' or 'sure, see you there'. If I am going to refuse, by contrast, I am unlikely to communicate that by just saying 'no, I can't' (let alone 'no, I don't want to').

Why the difference? Because refusing an invitation—even one that is much less sensitive than a sexual proposal—is a more delicate matter than accepting one. The act of inviting someone implies that you hope they will say yes: if they say no, there is a risk that you will be offended, upset, or just disappointed. To show that they are aware of this, and do not want you to feel bad, people generally design refusals to convey reluctance and regret. Compared to acceptances—which can be relatively brusque because they do not entail the same risk—refusals are elaborate and lengthy affairs, containing some or all of the following features:

1. A delay in responding, marked by a silent pause or an 'um' (whereas acceptances are usually delivered without hesitation).
2. A hedging expression, most commonly 'well'.
3. A 'softening' remark, like 'I'd love to, but . . .'.
4. An acceptable reason for refusing.

So, if you invite me to the pub and for whatever reason I do not want to come, what I am most likely to say is not 'no' (or even, 'no, sorry'), it is something like '(pause) well, I'd love to, but I promised I'd be home early tonight'.

Because this pattern is so consistent, and because it contrasts with the pattern for the alternative response, acceptance, refusals are immediately recognizable as such. In fact, the evidence suggests that people can tell a refusal is coming as soon as they register the initial hesitation. And when I say 'people', I mean people of both sexes. No one has found any difference between men's and women's use of the system I have just described.

As Kitzinger and Frith comment, this evidence undermines the claim that men do not understand any refusal less direct than a firm 'no'. If 'ordinary', non-sexual refusals do not generally take the form of saying 'no', but are performed using conventional strategies like hesitating, hedging, and offering excuses, then sexual refusals which use exactly the same strategies should not present any special problem. 'For men to claim that they do not understand such refusals to be refusals', Kitzinger and Frith say, 'is to lay claim to an astounding and implausible ignorance.'[10]

Even so, you might think that if a woman is worried about being assaulted she should err on the side of caution: forget the usual social niceties and 'unequivocally indicate a lack of willing participation'. The Canadian tribunal was clearly puzzled by MB's failure to do this. They pressed her about it until she finally offered an explanation. Like the women in Kitzinger and Frith's study, MB felt it was prudent to try to 'soften the blow'. She did not confront her assailant directly, she said, because she was afraid of him—and of what, beyond sexual assault, he might do to her if she provoked him.

> You do whatever you have to to survive. ((crying)) I mean I was just thinking how to survive that second. I mean I didn't care if that meant getting back into bed with him. If he didn't hurt me I didn't care at that second. . . . I did whatever I could to get by.

This raises doubts about the wisdom of expert advice on rape prevention, which tells women to do the opposite of 'softening the blow': in essence it tells them to aggravate the offence of rejecting a man's advances by verbalizing their refusals in a highly confrontational way. This advice presupposes that men who persist in making unwanted sexual advances are genuinely confused, and will be happy to have their confusion dispelled by a simple, firm 'no'. It does not allow for the possibility that men who behave in this way are not so much confused about women's wishes as indifferent to them. Confronting a violent and determined aggressor is not necessarily the safest option, and to a woman who is terrified it may well seem like the most dangerous, putting her at risk of being beaten as well as raped.

Women are not wrong to fear the consequences of following advice to 'just say no'. But thanks to the myth of Mars and Venus, they are not only receiving bad advice on how to prevent rape, they are also being held responsible for preventing it and blamed if they do not succeed.

✴ Failure to communicate?

The 1967 prison film *Cool Hand Luke* is remembered, among other things, for a line spoken by the prison warden to Luke, an inmate who persistently rebels against authority. 'What we have here', says the warden, 'is failure to communicate.' Both of them know that communication is not the issue. Luke understands the warden, but chooses to defy him. What the warden really means by 'failure to communicate' is 'failure to do what I want you to do'.

A similar (mis)use of the word 'communication' has become increasingly common in our culture. Conflicts which are really caused by people wanting different things (he wants her to have sex and she does not want to; she wants him to do his share of the housework and he wants her to stop nagging about it) are persistently described as 'misunderstandings' or 'communication problems'. If someone does not respond in the way we want them to, it means they cannot have understood us—the problem is 'failure to communicate', and the solution is better communication.

This belief, or hope, is undoubtedly one of the things that make the idea of male–female miscommunication appealing to many people. In the words of Deborah Tannen:[11]

> Understanding style differences for what they are takes the sting out of them. Believing that 'you're not interested in me', 'you don't care about me as much as I care about you' or 'you want to take away my freedom' feels awful. Believing that 'you have a different way of showing you're listening' or 'showing you care' allows for no-fault negotiation: you can ask for or make adjustments without casting or taking blame.

It is comforting to be told that nobody needs to 'feel awful': that there are no real conflicts, only misunderstandings, and no disagreements of substance, only differences of style. Acknowledging that many problems between men and women go deeper than 'failure to communicate' would make for a much bleaker and less reassuring message.

But the research evidence does not support the claims made by Tannen and others about the nature, the causes, and the prevalence of male–female miscommunication. No doubt some conflicts between individual men and women are caused by misunderstanding: the potential for communication to go awry is latent in every exchange between humans, simply because language is not telepathy. But the idea that men and women have a particular problem because they differ systematically in their ways of using language, and that this is the major source of conflict between them, does not stand up to scrutiny.

In this chapter and the last one, I have been considering a version of the myth of Mars and Venus which says that men and women communicate differently, and have difficulty understanding one another, because their formative years are spent in separate social worlds. There is also, however, a version of the story which traces the same differences back to the formation of the human species. In this version, our behaviour is not something we learn from our childhood playmates; it is something we inherit from our prehistoric ancestors. In the following chapter I will look in more detail at the idea that sex-differences in language and communication are innate, or in the currently fashionable phrase, 'hard-wired'.

6
Back to Nature:
Brains, Genes, and Evolution

In 2005, a headline in the London *Evening Standard* proclaimed: 'Men Are Better Shoppers than Women: It's in the Genes'. The story concerned a study of shopping patterns in fourteen different countries, which discovered that 'females tend to visit more shops than necessary, spend more time shopping than they need to and shop more often than they need to. Males try to complete their shopping in the shortest possible time.'[1]

The most obvious explanation of these findings is that women enjoy shopping more than men. But that was evidently too simple for the researchers:

Men are genetically programmed to be better shoppers than women. . . . Men's 'hunter-gatherer' inheritance means they are more effective at going in for the 'kill' on the high street—as they did on prehistoric plains millions of years ago. They spend less time browsing and have a far clearer idea of what they want. . . . Even men's heart rates increase at the moment of purchase, an echo of the excitement at the climax of a successful Stone Age hunt.[2]

Arguing that some apparently modern phenomenon, like shopping or eating junk food, can best be explained by going back to the Stone Age is the hallmark of a branch of science known as evolutionary psychology. According to evolutionary psychologists, many behaviour-patterns which we might assume to be products of culture are actually the results of biological evolution: they reflect the ways in which our earliest ancestors adapted to the conditions of life on the prehistoric plain. We no longer live in our ancestors' world, but we do inherit their genes: the qualities that served them well are now 'hard-wired' in us. Evolutionary psychologists also maintain that these qualities are different for men and women. Our ancestors had no concept of equal opportunities: the genes they have passed on to us make us different not just in the obvious physical ways, but also in the workings of our minds.

Some of the most important ways in which the minds of the sexes are said to differ relate to language and communication. According to the back cover of a popular science book called *Why Men Don't Iron: The Fascinating and Unalterable Differences between Men and Women*: 'Boys excel in tasks that require three-dimensional thought processing, girls in verbal skills. Men's brains are built for action and women's for talking: men do, women communicate.'[3]

Simon Baron-Cohen, author of *The Essential Difference*, offers a variation on this theme.[4] In his view, male brains are built to systemize (understand and put together complex systems), while female brains are built to empathize (understand and respond appropriately to the thoughts and feelings of others). Sex-differences in language and communication are a by-product of this deeper difference. Women's empathy with others is reflected in such familiar Venusian tendencies as the greater importance they attach to talking, their preference for a collaborative style of talk, and their tendency to talk about people and feelings. Men's aptitude for systemizing is reflected in their Martian preference for action over words, for instrumental, 'getting things done' talk, and for conversations about batting averages and the best route from A to B.

Why Men Don't Iron and *The Essential Difference* belong to a current of Mars and Venus literature which sets out to debunk the 'politically correct' idea that male–female differences are products of culture. The truth, it says, is that differences between men and women reflect innate biological factors: our genetic inheritance and the influence of sex-hormones on our brains. The reason, it adds, is that evolution favoured different abilities in Stone Age men and women.

But why was it advantageous to our prehistoric ancestors if women's brains were built for talking and men's for other purposes? I will return in a moment to the answers scientists have proposed. First, though, let us briefly consider a claim which is implicit in the question: that there are differences in the construction of men's and women's brains, which affect their linguistic behaviour.

✴ Sex, language, and the brain

Like most things about men and women, their brains are more similar than different. There are, however, some differences between the sexes, both in the anatomy of the brain and in the way it is organized for various functions, including language.

The evidence which suggests this comes from two main sources. One is the study of people with brain damage caused by head injuries, tumours, or strokes. By observing how the location of the injury relates to the type of impairment a person manifests, it is possible to infer which parts of the brain would normally be responsible for which functions. The other source is research using techniques like fMRI (functional magnetic resonance imaging). These techniques typically measure the blood flow in the brain when its owner is doing a particular task. Increased blood flow, implying increased activity, translates into a visual image that shows the active parts of the brain 'lighting up'.

Both kinds of evidence suggest that language may be more strongly lateralized in men's brains than in women's. The term 'lateralized' refers to the fact that the brain has two hemispheres, which specialize in different functions. Language is typically a left-hemisphere function. But the dominance of the left hemisphere seems to be stronger in men: women appear to make more use of both hemispheres.

This difference might help to explain the clinical observation that men are more vulnerable than women to aphasia (language loss) and other language impairments caused by brain injuries. Women who suffer damage to their left hemisphere are less likely to become aphasic than men who have sustained similar damage;[5] if their linguistic functioning is initially impaired, they have a better chance of recovery than similarly impaired men. This may be because in women there are areas in the right hemisphere which can take over the functions of the damaged part.

But it remains unclear why men and women who have not suffered any injury should apparently use different parts of their brains to carry out the same linguistic tasks. Though some scientists think this may be linked to women's superior verbal skills (others think it may be linked to men's superior spatial skills), research has not so far produced clear evidence to support these speculations. Some imaging studies have found that, on the contrary, whether a subject used one or both hemispheres to do a verbal task made no discernible difference to the outcome. Men who showed activity only in the left hemisphere were neither slower nor less accurate than women who showed activity in both hemispheres.[6]

Popular science writers who make sweeping claims like 'men's brains are built for action and women's for talking' are presenting as fact what is still largely a matter of speculation. There is a great deal we do not yet know about how the brain works and how a person's sex affects that. Even where there is agreement that a difference exists between men and women, there is often no consensus on how to explain it. And it is not only the less reputable popular writers who are sometimes driven to fill the gaps in our current knowledge with speculations whose scientific status is questionable.

✸ Stories and speculations

As I have already noted, contemporary scientists are drawn towards the kind of explanation which attributes the existence of sex-differences in modern humans to the adaptive value for survival which those differences had for their Stone Age ancestors. This kind of explanation is unavoidably speculative, because it depends on reconstructing the details of Stone Age life from the very limited evidence that survives. In the case of language, the evidence is not just limited, it is non-existent. Since early humans could not write, their languages (unlike, say, their tools and their art) have left no traces for modern science to study.

Many of the things which interest evolutionary psychologists (for instance, early humans' emotions, their sexual behaviour, and the way they cared for their children) are, like language, impossible to draw conclusions about from fossil remains and preserved artefacts. The scientists are obliged to construct narratives about our ancestors based on a mixture of what we think we do know about their lives, what we observe among modern humans (and sometimes other primate species), and what are understood to be general principles of evolution. At the same time, they assume that the behaviour of modern humans must be explained as a more-or-less direct continuation of what went on among prehistoric

105

ones. This somewhat circular reasoning can produce stories that strain credulity. When researchers propose that our approaches to shopping reflect traits inherited from Stone Age hunter-gatherers, it is hard not to be reminded of *The Flintstones*—the popular cartoon series about a 'modern Stone Age family' whose world is exactly like a 1960s American suburb except that they haven't yet invented the wheel.

An obvious question to ask about something like the shopping study is why the scientists feel the need for a biological, back-to-the-Stone-Age explanation. Wouldn't shopping be better explained as a cultural phenomenon? That question can also be asked about sex-differences in language. Language, admittedly, is a better candidate than shopping for the evolutionary approach. No one disputes that the human language faculty itself has a biological basis, and must therefore be a product of evolution. But it does not necessarily follow that differences in the way different groups of people *use* language must be expressions of innate characteristics. Eating and having sex are clearly things we are innately predisposed to do (their importance for survival is self-evident), but that does not mean people are hard-wired to indulge in fetishism or fine dining. These are more likely to be cultural elaborations, particularly as they are not found in all times and all places.

Language is a similar case: the capacity for it is certainly hard-wired, but our infinitely varied ways of using it need not be. So how do evolutionary psychologists justify their belief that male–female differences in language-use are not cultural elaborations, but biological imperatives with their roots in human prehistory?

★ Evolution, sex, and language

It is a basic assumption of evolutionary theory that there is no 'intelligent designer' directing the progress of organisms towards some predetermined goal. Evolution happens because in any population there will be genetic variations: over time some of these will spread at the expense of others because they prove to be advantageous for survival.

'Survival' in modern evolutionary theory means ensuring the survival of your genes by passing them on to offspring. To say that a gene is advantageous for survival is to say that individuals who possess it are more successful at reproducing themselves than those who do not. The drive to maximize reproductive success—pass your genes on to as many offspring as possible—is fundamental for both sexes. Evolutionary scientists argue, however, that the biological facts of sexual reproduction give it different implications for males and females.

In theory, there is virtually no limit to the number of offspring a human male can father. Females, on the other hand, can only conceive a certain number of times, and for them conception is only the beginning of a much longer process involving gestation, giving birth, and caring for a dependent infant. This restricts female sexual availability, making women a scarce resource which men must compete for. It also gives women a reason to be picky about who they mate with: for them every sexual encounter represents what could be a huge investment of time and energy. The result is that males do the courting, and females do the choosing.

Theorists reason that among our prehistoric ancestors, reproductive success demanded not only differences in the anatomy and physiology of the two sexes, but differences in their ways of thinking, feeling, and behaving. The most successful males were those who maximized their opportunities to mate—who were aggressive in competition with other males, and who possessed qualities (such as hunting skills) which females considered desirable. The most successful females, by contrast, were those who chose their mates wisely and nurtured their children well.

It is not hard to see how language might be incorporated into this picture. Socially skilled, nurturant women would also have been more fluent, articulate, and 'caring' communicators; men would have placed more emphasis on non-verbal abilities like those required to hunt, and their talk—when they did talk—would have reflected their generally competitive mentality. All of which is, of course, exactly what the myth of Mars and Venus says about male and female language-use today.

Many evolutionary scientists embrace the myth wholeheartedly. But they have different ways of weaving it into the larger story of the descent of Man and Woman. These differences are bound up with the answers they give to another big question about human evolution: how and why language itself evolved.

It might seem self-evident that the ability to speak would be an advantage in the struggle to survive and reproduce; but the advantages of any characteristic have to be set against the costs. In the case of language, the cost is heavy: to accommodate it, humans need very large brains. Large brains demand a lot of energy; they also take time to develop. Because their brains at birth are immature, human infants remain helpless and dependent for several years. What advantage could language have conferred on our species that outweighed these significant disadvantages?

✭ Gathering, mothering, and gossiping

In the past, it was often suggested that the big advantage conferred by language was that it enabled hunters to coordinate their activities more efficiently. Since hunters were assumed to be male, it followed that men were the driving force in the evolution of language. But the general assumptions of evolutionary psychology fit better with stories in which women were the driving force; today there are several competing stories of this kind.

One of these stories suggests that the main advantage language offered had to do with the management of social relationships in prehistoric human groups. Humans are social animals who survive by cooperating as well as competing. To succeed as a social animal it is necessary both to maintain social relationships and to keep track of them—you need to be aware of who is doing what with whom and where they are in the pecking order.

Our closest non-human relatives, apes, negotiate their relationships through grooming each other. But when a group gets beyond a certain size, one-to-one physical contact becomes a time-consuming and inefficient way of keeping up your social networks. According to the evolutionary scientist Robin Dunbar, this may have been a decisive factor in the evolution of language.[7] Dunbar believes that in the course of human evolution, environmental conditions made it advantageous for the size of the average human group to increase. As groups grew too large for grooming to be manageable, language provided a more efficient substitute. The ability to speak enabled people to maintain social relationships and exchange social information many-to-many as well as one-to-one. It also meant they could do it without having to put aside every other task (since unlike grooming, talking leaves your hands free).

In Dunbar's story, the primary purpose for which language was selected was to enable humans to gossip—that is, to engage in the kind of talk that conveys information about, and passes judgement on, the activities and relationships of group-members. He also argues that women rather than men were the driving force behind this development. Females are at the centre of most stable primate social networks, whereas males tend to be more peripheral. If that was also true of early human groups, the women would have been better placed to act as conduits for gossip.

Some stories which also accord women a primary role in language evolution give more weight to two other aspects of their roles in prehistoric society. Women were mothers, and would presumably have vocalized to the children they cared for. They were also gatherers rather than hunters. As one writer, Rhawn Joseph, summarizes:[8]

> Over the course of human evolution . . . female mothers and female gatherers were able to freely chatter with their babies or amongst themselves . . . Unlike the men who must remain quiet for long time periods in order to not scare off game, the women are free to chatter and talk to their hearts' delight.

Whereas gathering and childcare responsibilities allowed women to develop verbal skill, hunting inhibited this development in men because it required them to spend long periods without talking. What men needed to hunt successfully was not verbal skill but spatial skill—the ability to plan routes, judge distances, and calculate angles. This fits perfectly with what is claimed on the cover of *Why Men Don't Iron*—that among modern humans, 'boys excel in tasks that require three-dimensional thought processing, girls in verbal skills'. The Stone Age story explains both how that difference came into existence, and also why it became a hard-wired characteristic of the human species.

On closer inspection, though, there are reasons to doubt that this story explains much at all. To begin with, there is a logical problem: the so-called explanation presupposes what it is meant to be explaining. Modern women's superior verbal skills and modern men's superior spatial skills are explained by saying that prehistoric conditions favoured the development of just those skills in our ancestors: we modern humans have simply inherited them. But there is no independent evidence that early human females had superior verbal skills. The only evidence for the prehistoric sex-difference is the modern sex-difference which it is supposed to explain.

What about the argument that hunters (male) had to be silent whereas gatherers (female) were free to talk? Isn't that a point in favour of the theory? Maybe: but a lot of what is said about early humans is based on anthropological studies of groups who have maintained the hunter-gatherer way of life into modern times. And for these groups, 'men hunt, women gather' is now considered to be an oversimplification.[9] In general, it is gathering which provides the bulk of what modern hunter-gatherers subsist on. Gathering is a regular activity, and is often engaged in by both sexes, whereas hunting tends to be more sporadic. While it is typical for the hunting of large animals to be a male preserve, women do hunt smaller game.

In addition, hunting is something men generally do in groups. It needs planning and coordination, and often involves lengthy periods spent travelling to where the animals are. Some hunters have been observed to perform rituals at the site of a kill, and to spend time butchering and partially consuming the meat before beginning the journey back. If we assume (as evolutionary psychologists usually do) that early human practices were similar to those of hunter-gatherer peoples today, it does not seem plausible to claim that their role as hunters deprived prehistoric men of opportunities to talk. It seems more likely that hunting expeditions were not an everyday occurrence, and that when they did take place they were occasions for male bonding, in which verbal interaction played a part.

✶ Lekking and listening

Some evolutionary scientists tell a different story about how and why language evolved: they suggest that it was a product of 'sexual selection'. Sexual selection is the concept which explains why some characteristics get selected despite the fact that they do not have any obvious survival value. They may even appear to be counterproductive—the peacock's large and gaudy tail, for instance, makes it more conspicuous to predators. The theory of sexual selection proposes that these characteristics do have a value: they make their possessors more attractive to the opposite sex and thus enable them to mate more often. It is not a coincidence that many of them are specifically male characteristics (like bright plumage or large horns). This is linked to the principle that males court and females choose. The lavishly ornamented peacock's tail says to peahens: 'choose me!'

It would be hard to argue that language was purely ornamental, but some theorists do argue that if utility had been the only consideration, we could have got by with something much less elaborate. Human verbal abilities go far beyond what is needed for efficient communication, and in that sense do not justify their high cost. Their selection might be explicable, however, if the capacity for language also made individuals more attractive to potential mates—if it gave human males a new and powerful tool for advertising themselves to human females.

Robin Dunbar (who believes that this self-advertising function was a by-product of the evolution of language rather than the main purpose for which it evolved) cites an interesting finding as evidence for this theory.[10] His research on present-day humans found that although both sexes spent much the same amount of time exchanging social information, men spent more time than women talking about themselves, as opposed to about other people. Dunbar explains this as a form of what is called 'lekking' in peacocks and certain other species. The lek is a kind of courtship ritual in which males display themselves and females select the best ones to mate with.

This account seems to overlook the fact that modern advice on human courtship consistently recommends showing an interest in the other person as a more effective strategy than talking endlessly about yourself. Leaving that detail aside, however, what is most puzzling about the self-advertisement theory is its apparent incompatibility with the idea that women are more verbally skilled than men. If language enabled prehistoric men to show off to their womenfolk, shouldn't verbal skill be a guy thing?

This contradiction is inventively addressed by Geoffrey Miller, a scholar who believes that language, art, and culture evolved mainly as tools for courtship (for him the principle that males court and females choose explains why most of the world's art and public culture has been produced by men).[11]

He gets over the objection that in that case men should be the more verbal sex by suggesting that the main area in which women's linguistic abilities outstrip men's is not talking but *listening*.[12] Women evolved into the proverbial 'good listeners' because they spent millennia judging the quality of men's verbal displays in order to choose the best mates to father their children.

This claim underscores a problem with evolutionary psychology which I have already drawn attention to—the inherently speculative nature of its arguments. These are often ingenious, but in the absence of direct evidence about prehistoric language-use, impossible to verify or falsify. There are too many different and incompatible stories that can be made to fit the supposed facts—especially if, like many of the writers I have mentioned, you approach the (modern) evidence like a peahen at a lek, fastening enthusiastically on the splashiest generalizations while disregarding the more serviceable but drabber specimens.

✴ Factual selection?

The argument that a sex-difference is 'in the genes' will always be stronger if the difference in question appears consistently across a wide range of cultures and in different historical eras. If it is variable in time and space, that suggests that it is more likely to reflect social and cultural factors. The way evolutionary psychologists talk about sex-differences in language implies that they think the Mars and Venus generalizations they use to back up their story—for instance that women like to talk more than men, have better verbal skills than men, are less competitive and less direct in their speech than men, and so on—apply, if not universally, then very widely across cultures. But if that is what they think, they are overlooking a fair amount of evidence to the contrary.

In Chapter 2 we visited the people of Gapun, in Papua New Guinea, and the Malagasy people of the island of Madagascar —two of many non-western societies in which the stereotypical Mars and Venus patterns are absent or reversed. Women are more assertive and more direct in their speech than men; men are believed by both sexes to be more verbally skilled than women, largely because of their greater facility with the highly elaborate language used on ritual occasions.

For evolutionary psychologists trying to argue that certain patterns of linguistic behaviour reflect innate characteristics, the existence of such striking cross-cultural variation is a problem in itself. But the form that variation takes is arguably an even bigger problem. Evolutionary psychologists usually reason that the less a society has been affected by very recent cultural and technological developments, the more it should be able to tell us about the lives and behaviour of ancestral humans. On that reasoning, the pattern of sex-differences found in more traditional societies should be a better model for reconstructing prehistory than patterns which—like modern industrial society itself—may only go back a couple of centuries. (As well as having evidence of cross-cultural variation in patterns of gender difference, we have evidence that those patterns have varied historically: some male–female differences which are reported consistently in modern western speech communities apparently did not exist in the same communities in earlier periods.[13])

Their failure to deal with the cross-cultural and historical evidence is not the only respect in which evolutionary psychologists are selective in their use of research. Most versions of the Stone Age narrative assume that females have superior verbal skills, and that their story needs to explain that. But the research evidence suggests that they are over-explaining it: sex-differences in verbal ability are really not very large. In Chapter 3 I quoted one linguist's estimate that the overlap between men and women is about 99.75 per cent.

Another generalization which is often used to support the thesis that 'men's brains are built for action and women's for talking' is that women talk more than men. According to Rhawn Joseph, they inherit their loquacity from prehistoric women who were 'free to chatter and talk to their heart's delight'. But the idea of the 'chattering' woman is a stereotype which research has repeatedly contradicted.

In Chapter 1, I discussed the claim that the average woman utters 20,000 words in a day to the average man's 7,000. As we saw, these figures were based on no reliable evidence, and in any case there is too much variation among individuals to make an average male or female daily word-count meaningful. If we are going to try to generalize about which sex talks more, a more reliable way to do it is to observe both sexes in a single interaction, and measure their respective contributions.

This cuts out extraneous variables that are likely to affect the amount of talk (like whether someone is spending their day at a Buddhist retreat or a high school reunion), and allows for a comparison of male and female behaviour under the same contextual conditions.

Numerous studies have been done using this approach, and while as always, the results have been mixed, by far the commonest finding is that men talk more than women. One review of fifty-six research studies categorizes their findings as shown in Table 2.

The reviewers are inclined to believe that this is a case of the 'missing link' phenomenon I explained in Chapter 3. Gender and amount of talk are linked indirectly rather than directly: the more direct link is with status, in combination with the formality of the setting (status tends to be more relevant in formal situations). The basic trend, especially in formal and public contexts, is for higher-status speakers to talk more than lower-status ones. The gender pattern is explained by the

Table 2

Pattern of difference found	Number of studies
Men talk more than women	34 (60.8%)
Women talk more than men	2 (3.6%)
Men and women talk the same amount	16 (28.6%)
No clear pattern	4 (7.0%)

Source: based on Deborah James and Janice Drakich, 'Understanding Gender Differences in Amount of Talk', in Deborah Tannen (ed.), *Gender and Conversational Interaction* (New York: Oxford University Press, 1993), 281–312.

observation that in most contexts where status is relevant, men are more likely than women to occupy high-status positions; if all other things are equal, gender itself is a hierarchical system in which men are regarded as having higher status.

'Regarded' is an important word here, because conversational dominance is not just about the way dominant speakers behave; it is also about the willingness of others to defer to them. Some experimental studies have found that you can reverse the 'men talk more' pattern, or at least reduce the gap, by instructing subjects to discuss a topic which both sexes consider a distinctively female area of expertise. In a discussion of fashion, or pregnancy, men will more readily cede the floor to women. Status, then, is not a completely fixed attribute, but can vary relative to the setting, subject, and purpose of conversation.

That may be why some studies find that women talk more in domestic interactions with partners and family members: in the domestic sphere, women are often seen as being in charge. In other spheres, however, the default assumption is that men outrank women, and men are usually found to talk more. In informal contexts where status is not an issue, the commonest finding is not that women talk more than men, it is that the two sexes contribute about equally.

If it does not reflect reality, why is the folk-belief that women talk more than men so persistent? The feminist Dale Spender once suggested an explanation: she said that people overestimate how much women talk because they think that ideally, women would not talk at all.[14] While that may be rather sweeping, it is true that belief in female loquacity is generally combined with disapproval of it. The statement 'women talk more than men' tends to imply the judgement 'women talk too much'. (As one old proverb charmingly puts it: 'Many women, many words; many geese, many turds.')

The folk-belief that women talk more than men persists because it provides a justification for an ingrained social prejudice. Evolutionary psychology is open to a similar criticism: that it takes today's social prejudices and projects them back into prehistory, thus elevating them to the status of timeless truths about the human condition.

Champions of the evolutionary approach often say it is their opponents whose arguments are based on prejudice rather than facts or logic. They complain that feminists and other 'PC' types are unwilling even to consider the idea that sex-differences might have biological rather than social causes. Instead of judging the arguments on their merits, these politically motivated critics just denounce them, and those who advance them, as reactionary and bigoted.

Whether biological explanations of male–female differences are inherently more problematic than cultural explanations is a perennial question, and I will return to it in the concluding chapter. In this chapter, however, I have attempted to examine the arguments using the same criteria I applied to the 'cultural' arguments discussed in earlier chapters. If I have failed to find much merit in them, it is not simply because they are about genes and brain-wiring. My main criticism of the evolutionary story is exactly the same one I have already made of the story told by writers like Deborah Tannen, who do not favour biological explanations. Both stories have the same basic flaw: they are based not on facts, but on myths.

In the next chapter I will turn to an area of modern life where myths about the way men and women communicate are both widespread and consequential: the public sphere of work and politics.

7

Public Speaking:
Mars and Venus in Politics and the Workplace

In 2006, Tony Blair, the Prime Minister and leader of Britain's Labour Party, told the House of Commons that the next election would be a contest between 'a heavyweight and a flyweight'. He predicted that his successor Gordon Brown would knock out the Conservative leader David Cameron with a 'big clunking fist'. These remarks delighted the Cameron camp while appalling many on Blair's own side. Labour supporters feared for their electoral prospects if voters got the idea that, as one journalist put it, 'Gordon Brown is from Mars, David Cameron is from Venus'.[1]

Today it is a truism that effective leaders do not use 'big clunking fists': in the words of management guru Tom Peters, they 'listen, motivate, support'. They wear their authority lightly and are not afraid to show their feelings. David Cameron personifies this new Venusian style of leadership, and that was probably an important reason why his party, out of power for a decade and trying desperately to modernize its image, chose him as its leader over older and more experienced candidates.

But Cameron is also a typical Venusian leader in another, more paradoxical way: he is a man. Women may be the sex that comes from Venus, but they are still infrequent visitors to the realms of power. No British political party is currently led by a woman (the only woman ever to lead her party was Margaret Thatcher, who was definitely not from Venus). In business it has been estimated that women hold just 10 per cent of non-executive directorships and a mere 3 per cent of executive ones.[2] From trade unions to academe, and from the police force to the media, the story is the same. The further up the hierarchy you go, the more men outnumber and outrank women.

There is a long-standing belief that these facts might be explained in part by differences between male and female styles of communication. It is argued that women's preference for cooperative and relational ways of interacting puts them at a disadvantage in the public sphere, whose norms are more competitive and instrumental. Women are said to have difficulty in exercising authority directly, in acting decisively, and in dealing with aggression or conflict. They may be seen as good lieutenants, but not as potential commanders-in-chief. They are also said to lose out to men because they are too reticent about their own achievements. While competitive men are busy blowing their own trumpets, supportive women are sharing the credit and missing out on the rewards they deserve.

In the 1970s and 1980s, before the ascendancy of the current myth of Mars and Venus, these ideas were framed by a 'deficit model' of gender difference. Men's behaviour was the norm, and women were deficient by comparison. A flourishing genre of advice literature argued that if women wanted to get ahead, they must make themselves more like men. A 1989 book entitled *Leadership Skills for Women* counselled: 'men typically use less body language than women: watch their body language to see how they do it'.[3] The authors saw no need to explain why 'less' body-language would be preferable to 'more'. In professional contexts, men's ways of doing things were axiomatically preferable to women's.

If this sort of advice is now as unfashionable as a 1980s shoulder pad, that is because the deficit model has been largely superseded. The myth of Mars and Venus does not say that women are deficient: it says they are 'different but equal'. In fact, women are often described in terms that suggest they are more than equal. The literature of management, both expert and popular, is full of statements like the following:

> A woman's leadership style is transformational and inter-personal, while a man's style is based on command and control. Women managers promote positive interactions with subordinates, encourage participation and share power and information more than men do . . . Women leaders use collaborative, participative communication that enables and empowers others, while men use more unilateral, directive communication.[4]

In this, the business world's version of the myth of Mars and Venus, it is noticeable that all the modern management buzzwords—*transformational*, *positive*, *participation*, *enable*, *empower*—are applied to women. Men are associated with the 'command and control' approach which management gurus have spent the last fifteen years decrying. This rhetoric makes you wonder why women are not at the helm of every successful business. On the assumption that the writer must know they are not, it also makes you wonder how, if pressed, she would explain that.

My own explanation would be that Mars and Venus generalizations about gender and management or leadership styles cannot explain reality because they do not describe reality. They are sweeping, inaccurate, and simplistic. All they do is reinforce the attitudes and practices which are at the root of women's continuing difficulty in gaining access to positions of power. In support of this argument, I want to look at some research which has examined the way men and women really communicate in public settings. But before I turn to contemporary research, a brief historical detour is in order.

★ Private women, public men

The dominance of men in powerful positions is a historical legacy of the old doctrine of 'separate spheres', which effectively excluded women from most areas of public life. That exclusion had a linguistic dimension: one way in which it was maintained was through a specific prohibition on women speaking in public. For respectable Victorians, the idea of women making political speeches, giving lectures, or preaching sermons was not merely incongruous ('like a dog walking on its hind legs', as Dr Johnson had said of women preachers a century earlier), it was scandalous. In 1837, a group of Congregationalist ministers published a letter in which they declared that a woman who spoke in public would 'not only cease to bear fruit [i.e., become infertile], but fall in shame and dishonor in the dust'.[5] These reverend gentlemen were by no means alone in seeing precious little difference between public speaking and prostitution.

Nineteenth-century women who wanted to address audiences in public, whether for political reasons or as a way of making a living, had to find ways around these punitive attitudes. Many adopted a very conservative style of dress to deflect the criticism that they were making a sexual spectacle of themselves. Some sought to defuse religious objections by comparing themselves to the female prophets of the Old Testament. Emma Willard, who undertook a speaking tour of the US in 1846, hit on the strategy of lecturing from a chair instead of a podium. This gesture redefined what was really a public lecture as something closer to the domestic genre of private conversation, and thereby rendered it more acceptable.

Victorian attitudes may seem ridiculous to us today, but old prejudices die hard. Although women are no longer forbidden to speak in public settings, it is still common for them to feel, or be made to feel, like interlopers when they do. That has implications for the way women communicate, as we will see if we consider the case of women MPs in the British House of Commons.

✴ Women, the interlopers

The debating chamber of House of Commons is a peculiarly Martian institution. Not only has it always been dominated by men (women were excluded until the twentieth century, and have never made up more than about a fifth of the total membership), it is world-famous for the extremely adversarial style of politics that is practised in it.

Officially, arcane rules of courtesy govern the speech of MPs. They are not allowed to address each other directly, but must address their remarks to the Speaker and refer to other members in the third person using formulas like 'my honourable friend' or 'the honourable member'. If they wish to speak when they have not been called by the Speaker, they must request the current speaker to 'give way', and desist from speaking if he or she declines to do so. Speech is only 'legal' if delivered from a standing position. Calling out comments from your seat is in theory a breach of the rules.

But in reality the rules are breached constantly. MPs yell, hoot, call out comments from their seats, and laugh uproariously at comments called out by their colleagues. Even when the rules are being observed, there is a great deal of verbal sparring of the kind Tony Blair was engaged in when he delivered his 'big clunking fist' remark. Although MPs can be censured for using 'unparliamentary language'—they may not, for example, swear or call one another liars—this does not prevent them from hurling taunts and insults, it just challenges them to formulate their verbal abuse more inventively.

Not everyone admires this knockabout style of politics. The influx of over 100 women MPs in 1997 prompted many media commentators, and some of the new MPs themselves, to suggest that women would exert a positive influence by introducing a more civilized way of doing business. There would be less shouting and more listening, less point-scoring and more consensus-building.

In 1999 the linguist Sylvia Shaw decided to investigate whether any of this was happening.[6] She found that it was not: rather than changing the verbal culture of the House of Commons, women seemed to have adjusted to its adversarial norms. In proportion to their numbers, women spoke as often as men and challenged other speakers to 'give way' as readily as men. In short, they were (as MPs at Westminster have to be) assertive in competing for opportunities to speak. There was, however, one significant difference. Women rarely seized the floor 'illegally' by interrupting or interjecting comments. In five debates analysed closely by Shaw, men made almost ten times as many illegal interventions as women. If these were counted alongside legal turns, women's overall contribution shrank to two-thirds of the men's total.

This, Shaw suggested, put women at a disadvantage, because taking turns illegally is a powerful strategy. It enhances MPs' reputations as effective Parliamentarians, and draws the attention of the senior politicians who are in a position to advance their careers. It can also influence the course of a debate. Illegal turns are strictly speaking 'out of order', and are not recorded in official proceedings; but what has been heard cannot be unheard, and in practice the 'legal' speaker often feels impelled to respond. Women MPs, by not interrupting, are denying themselves both visibility and influence.

Why do women behave in this way? Some told Shaw that they did not join in the collective cheering and jeering because they considered it 'puerile'. In other cases, though, women avoided breaking the rules because they feared being censured by the Speaker or other MPs. This was not just a case of women being oversensitive. Shaw's analysis suggested that women really were more likely than men to be censured for certain kinds of rule-breaking. In addition, both she and the authors of a later research report[7] found that women speakers were often subjected to sexist verbal harassment. Though barracking is an occupational hazard for anyone who speaks in a House of Commons debate, male MPs are not assailed by crude remarks and 'melon weighing' gestures alluding to their breasts. Many women reported that this behaviour made them think twice about drawing attention to themselves.

Women MPs are classic 'interlopers': they form a relatively small minority within a historically male institution, and the verbal harassment they face suggests a degree of active hostility to their presence. One logical response to being positioned as an interloper is to do exactly what Sylvia Shaw found the women MPs did: observe the rules meticulously as a symbolic way of showing that you are worthy to belong. Paradoxically, however, this strategy only underlines the insecurity of those who use it. Real insiders are not so punctilious: they have the confidence to break the rules.

Shaw also studied the recently opened Scottish Parliament, where once again, the most effective speakers tended to be people who deviated from the official rules. In Edinburgh, however, these rule-breakers were as likely to be women as men. This, Shaw argued, reflected the fact that the Scottish Parliament was a new institution, with procedures designed deliberately to be less arcane than Westminster's. The proportion of women members was higher, and they had been there from the very beginning.

The women MPs' problem is clearly not that they have a less assertive or competitive style of speaking than men. That would not explain why there is a difference between the Westminster and Edinburgh parliaments, nor why Westminster women hold their own with men so long as they are speaking legally. The variable that does explain these patterns is not gender as such, but whether or not women are positioned as interlopers. To the extent that their behaviour is different from men's, it is not because they have a different style, but because they have a different status.

Is this specifically a female problem, or are things the same for men who enter historically female domains? Because they have dominated most public settings, men are less often in this situation. But in any case, interloper status is not just the automatic consequence of being numerically in the minority: it is bound up with wider issues of power.

The exclusion of women from the public sphere was both a consequence and a reinforcement of their subordinate status. Their attempts to enter institutions such as higher education, politics, medicine, the Church, and the skilled craft trades were often resisted in part because of men's fear that women's presence would downgrade the institution's status. Men entering female domains do not usually encounter the same resistance, because women are not in the same position of defending their historic privileges against the incursions of a lower-status group. (In nursing, for example, men have been welcomed: their presence is felt to raise the status of the profession, and in proportion to their numbers they are over-represented in the highest grades.)

✭ Women, the carers

Sometimes, as in the House of Commons, women's entry into a high-status male institution is conditional on playing by the same rules as men. But in other cases, women may find that they are expected to be different, and judged harshly if they are not different enough. Even when they are doing exactly the same jobs as men, it may not be acceptable for women to do them in the same ways.

The linguist Clare Walsh studied the case of priests in the Church of England.[8] Anglican women won the right to be ordained as priests in 1994, following a long and acrimonious battle which was fought partly on the terrain of Mars and Venus. Supporters of women's ordination had argued that women were needed in the priesthood because they would bring something to their ministry that men could not: a distinctively female form of priesthood, based on the quasi-maternal qualities of caring and nurturance. This argument helped to achieve the immediate goal of opening up the priesthood to women, but it had consequences for the way they were treated once inside.

Walsh observed an emerging division of labour whereby women priests were channelled into pastoral work—tasks like visiting the sick and comforting the bereaved—while men dominated the activities and forms of speech that made them visible (and audible) in leadership roles, like chairing parish meetings and preaching at services. Though many of the women actively wanted to make the pastoral side of the job a priority, they had not expected to be confined to it; and they soon found that this did not advance their careers.

Though the priests are an extreme example, women in many professions find that they are cast in the role of carers. In teaching, for instance, it is commonly assumed that women will be the ones who deal with students' personal problems. Disciplining students, by contrast, is often left to men, who are seen as authority figures rather than carers. In politics, too, women often get the 'softer' ministerial portfolios—education and health rather than defence or trade or justice. A version of the traditional division between public men and private women thus gets recycled in the public sphere itself.

This may have a bearing on the claim that men and women have different styles of leadership. According to the expert I quoted earlier, 'women leaders use collaborative, participative communication that enables and empowers others, while men use more unilateral, directive communication'. If so, is that because of women's own aptitudes and preferences, or is it because they are expected to lead in a way that is 'caring' rather than authoritative? We will return to this question, but first we need to ask another: is it actually true that men and women do leadership differently?

✱ 'It's a royal no': the problem of female authority

That question has recently been investigated in some detail by the Wellington (New Zealand) Language in the Workplace Project. Between 1996 and 2003, a team directed by the linguist Janet Holmes recorded and analysed around 2,500 workplace interactions, involving over 500 people in twenty-two different private and public sector workplaces, with a particular focus on male and female managers.

The project did not find any clear-cut difference between male and female communication styles at work. As usual, the researchers found there was a great deal of intra-group variation: both male and female managers used a wide range of styles. There were men in the sample whose style was collaborative and supportive; there were women whose style was extremely directive.

Below I reproduce an extract from the transcript of a team meeting which was recorded for the New Zealand project.[9] The participants, four men and four women working for a multinational company, are considering whether users of a new computer process should be allowed to 'screendump', i.e. print material directly from the computer screen.

Harriet: looks like there's actually been a request for screen-dumps I know it was outside of the scope but people will be pretty worried about it

Clara: no screendumps

Peg: (sarcastically) thank you Clara

Clara: no screendumps

Matt: we know we know you didn't want them and we um er we've—

Clara: that does not meet the criteria

Smithy: so that's a clear well maybe no

Clara: it's a no

Smithy: it's a no a royal no

Clara, the leader of this team, could not be described as 'us[ing] collaborative and participative communication that enables and empowers others'. Though several members of her team are clearly unhappy with her decision, she dismisses their objections, twice, with a direct and decisive 'no screen-dumps'. She ignores Peg's sarcasm, cuts off Matt's attempt to argue, and puts Smithy firmly in his place when he suggests that her 'no' might mean 'maybe'. In short, her style is the 'unilateral and directive' one which the management liter-ature associates with men.

But what are we to make of Smithy's last remark, 'it's a no, a royal no'? Janet Holmes explains that Clara's team have evolved a way of dealing with her: they have cast her as 'Queen Clara'. The idea of Clara as a royal personage issuing orders from on high has become a running joke; Clara herself plays along with it, as the following extract shows (it was recorded as the team were waiting for a meeting to begin. 'XF' means that the voice on the recording belongs to an unidentified female):[10]

Smithy: how's your mum?
Clara: sorry?
Smithy: she broke her hip didn't she?
Clara: my mother? what are you talking about?
XF: (laughing) the queen mother
Clara: oh (putting on posh accent) my husband and I are confident she'll pull through

Holmes remarks that Clara is able to operate effectively because she combines her authority with self-deprecating humour. But we might ask: would a man in Clara's position who behaved in a similar way have to make the same concession? Would he be dubbed 'the King' by his subordinates, and teased about his 'royal' manner? Arguably, the humorous 'Queen Clara' persona is needed to render Clara's style of management acceptable precisely because she is not a man. A woman who displays authority as unabashedly as Clara still makes a lot of people feel uncomfortable or threatened.

★ Not all about gender

Another directive woman in the New Zealand sample is Ginette, the supervisor of a factory production team. In this extract she is talking to Russ, one of the packers she supervises.[11]

Russ: can you get me one please :*fa'amolemole*: [Samoan for 'please']

Ginette: you get one

Russ: ah you're not doing anything

Ginette: you go and get one

Russ: fuck it fuck you go get your fucking legs out here

Ginette: why didn't you get one before? I talked to you about that yesterday

It would be easy to interpret this exchange as a case of a man showing total disrespect for a woman's authority; but that would be to overlook the wider context. Ginette's workplace is a blue-collar environment, where arguing, complaining, and swearing are unremarkable (it is noticeable that Ginette does not react with shock or outrage when Russ swears at her). In a white-collar workplace like Clara's, by contrast, repeated swearing by either sex would be unacceptable; even the direct way Clara issues instructions or expresses disagreement ('no screendumps . . . it's a no') is evidently considered unusually blunt.

This example points to another problem with generalizations like 'women at work are unassertive', or 'women have problems giving direct orders'. These claims often equate 'women' with a very specific group of women, namely managers and other professionals who either are white and middle class, or are working in organizations whose culture is white and middle class. Though a disproportionate number of studies have focused on this group, it needs to be remembered that they are a minority. At work as elsewhere, differences of class, race, ethnicity, and culture make a difference to what is seen as 'normal' behaviour for women or men.

As part of a study of African American women's attitudes to hair, Lanita Jacobs-Huey recorded the speech of a number of black women hair-care professionals. These women typically had a very direct and assertive way of interacting, both with their co-workers and their clients. In the following extract, Carol and Gwen are leading a seminar for other salon owners:[12]

Carol: First of all I always tell my clients, 'you got to come to me to get your hair conditioned the right way . . . you can't do what I do because I'm licensed. That's what I do. I'm a hairstylist. You're the client'. You have to keep them in their spot

Gwen: their proper place

Carol: Let them know, 'I'm running this. That's my head!' (laughing) *So that's my head*

Gwen: You're in charge of that

Carol: and that's what they pay you for. You have to really take charge and show them you know that 'this is my head' but they'll respect you for it . . .

Carol and Gwen assert their professional authority directly and unapologetically, telling their audience what 'you have to' do and urging them to take the same approach with their own clients. These women belong to a community which values assertive speech-styles and does not define assertiveness as incompatible with femininity. As successful businesswomen in a black and female-dominated sector, they do not have to defer to anyone else's norms.

Another thing that affects the nature of workplace communication is the nature of the work itself. The linguistic anthropologist Bonnie McElhinny conducted research with police officers in the US city of Pittsburgh following an initiative to recruit more officers from under-represented groups, including women.[13] Like Sylvia Shaw in the British House of Commons, McElhinny found that women had adjusted to the communicative norms which were already in place. One adjustment they had made was to adopt a less emotionally expressive way of communicating: for instance, they maintained a level, neutral tone of voice and avoided smiling. To outside observers, these women's style came across as 'masculine'. But they did not see it that way: they pointed out that emotional inexpressiveness served a clear purpose, for both sexes, in the context of police work. In highly charged and potentially dangerous situations, it sent the message that officers were calm and in control.

Other jobs make different demands. Since the 1980s, more and more organizations have implemented 'customer care' policies which require workers not merely to provide a service, but to do it in a way that will make the recipient feel good. To that end, the use of language in many service workplaces is now intensively regulated. In the late 1990s I investigated the rules employees had to follow in a number of British call centres. I found that the prescribed style—for both sexes—was stereotypically 'feminine'.[14] Both workers' words and their tone of voice were required to communicate positive feelings like enthusiasm, cheerfulness, friendliness, and helpfulness. Workers were instructed to smile, use the caller's name, build rapport by making small-talk, listen actively, and give empathetic responses.

Unsurprisingly, I also found (as have numerous other researchers) that employers considered women to be more capable than men of meeting these demands. However, my own observations did not suggest that men working in call centres were any less skilled than women in the verbal art of customer care. Those I saw and spoke to had a similar attitude to the Pittsburgh women police officers: accepting that a certain way of speaking came with the territory, they just gritted their teeth (or rather, bared them in a smile) and got on with it.

✴ Danger: myth-making at work

Applied to the workplace and other public settings, the myth of Mars and Venus has real and potentially damaging consequences. Most obviously, it can be invoked to justify discrimination and double standards. In Chapter 1, for instance, I quoted a call centre manager who admitted to an interviewer: 'we do select women sometimes just because they are women'—a reference to his belief that women are better at customer care. Conversely, women who want to become MPs often complain that local party associations have a tendency to prefer male candidates because they believe women are less effective public speakers.

This kind of discrimination is based on beliefs about male–female differences which are not borne out by the evidence. The evidence suggests that you cannot predict an individual's communication style from their gender: there is too much overlap between men and women, and too much variation within each group. Of course there are women who fit the generalizations, but there are also many who do not. The Claras and Ginettes, the women MPs, police officers, and African American salon-owners, are too numerous to be dismissed as merely marginal exceptions.

Where gender differences do exist, the myth of Mars and Venus tends to obscure the underlying reasons for them. It makes the common-sense assumption that the way men and women communicate is just a reflection of the way men and women 'are'. Their communication styles are an integral part of them, like their blood group or their eye colour. But this is at best an oversimplification. It overlooks the rather obvious point that communication by definition involves more than one person. The way I speak to you is affected by the way you speak to me—and by my assessment of what you want from me, expect of me, or assume about me.

Whether or not women have any underlying disposition to behave differently from men, they are often obliged to be different because of other people's expectations. Emma Willard did not lecture sitting down because her natural modesty prevented her from standing: remaining seated was a tactical concession to prevailing notions of acceptable female conduct. Women MPs do not stick to the rules because they are timid conformists: they do it to counter the perception that they are interlopers. These ways of behaving are problem-solving strategies which women adopt in particular circumstances. They have nothing to do with the way women 'are', and everything to do with the position women are put in.

This is the issue that really needs to be addressed if women are to participate in public life on equal terms. The problem is not that men and women have different communication styles, but that whatever style women use, they are liable to be judged by different standards. Women are obliged to walk what Janet Holmes calls a 'tightrope of impression management',[15] continually demonstrating their professional competence while also making clear that they have not lost their femininity—that they are not, for example, aggressive or uncaring.

As Holmes points out, many women do walk the tightrope successfully; but negotiating such contradictory demands is an additional burden they have to carry. The myth of Mars and Venus only adds to women's load. By constantly drawing attention to their supposed difference, the myth helps to maintain the prejudices that are ultimately responsible for making women unequal.

8
Doing What Comes Culturally:
Gender, Identity, and Style

In Japan in the 1880s, people began to comment disapprovingly on a strange new way of talking that was popular among young women.[1] Just as today's English-speaking teenagers annoy their elders with their constant use of 'like' and 'y'know', Japanese girls in the late nineteenth century were accused of sprinkling their speech with the particles *teyo* and *dawa*. Commentators gave this style the label 'schoolgirl language'.

At the time, schoolgirls were a novel social category in Japan. Until 1879, the few girls who were sent to school at all had been educated exactly as if they were boys; they even dressed in schoolboys' clothing. But in 1879 the Emperor had decreed that girls should have their own schools. They should be given a distinctively female education, designed to prepare them for their future roles as 'good wives and wise mothers'.

In the wake of this change, fiction featuring schoolgirl characters had become popular. The stories, generally written by men, often had a moral agenda, pitting serious 'good girls'—those who aspired to become good wives and wise mothers—against shallow and frivolous 'bad girls'. The moral failings of the bad characters were signalled, among other things, by the frequency of *teyo* and *dawa* in the dialogue authors gave them. Virtuous characters, by contrast, did not use the particles at all. This was originally a fictional convention, created before actual schoolgirls had developed any particular way of talking. But over time, life imitated art. Real schoolgirls who read the stories began to use the particles as frequently as their imaginary counterparts.

Why did a convention invented by male fiction-writers have such an effect on the behaviour of young women? Probably because many girls did not wholeheartedly embrace the 'good-wife-wise-mother' ideal that was constantly emphasized in their schooling. When they read schoolgirl stories they identified with the 'bad' characters, the ones who did not conform to the ideal. Adopting these characters' style of speaking was a way of symbolizing a rebellious attitude: good girls were boring, bad girls were cool.

✷ Function and fashion

The myth of Mars and Venus generally explains the way men and women talk by saying that each sex is just doing what comes naturally. Differences in men's and women's ways of speaking are direct reflections of more fundamental differences in the two sexes' innate abilities ('men's brains are built for action and women's for talking'), their psychological make-up ('men are competitive, women are cooperative'), or the functions talking fulfils for them ('men talk to exchange information, women to make connections').

But this way of linking language to gender does not explain the emergence of *teyo* and *dawa* as features of female speech in nineteenth-century Japan. 'Schoolgirl language' was certainly not considered a sign of cooperativeness, empathy, or politeness: on the contrary, it was criticized as rebellious and disrespectful. Nor did it fulfil any obvious communicational need. It was a fictional convention, created originally by male writers; it was picked up from fiction by some young women students, who were then copied by others. It was, in short, a fashion, which spread in much the same way and for much the same reasons as other fashions do.

Whether an innovation catches on, and with whom, has a lot to do with the status of the people who adopt it first. If the coolest girls in the class start wearing a certain style of clothing or using a certain style of speech, that style is likely to be copied by other girls who want to be cool. At the same time, it will not be copied—it may even be actively resisted—by those who do not aspire to be like the cool girls. The linguist Mary Bucholtz studied a group of 'nerd girls' in California who defined themselves in conscious opposition to what their non-nerd peers considered 'cool': they used a very 'correct' and formal kind of speech to symbolize the value they accorded to knowledge and intellect, and they avoided the slang expressions favoured by other teenage girls.[2] Similarly, there were doubtless female students in 1880s Japan who did not adopt the fashion for saying *teyo* and *dawa*. And clearly, most boys did not adopt this fashion either, because it was strongly associated with girls.

Trying to explain the gender-specific use of *teyo* and *dawa* as a reflection of 'deeper' differences in the minds of men and women is like trying to explain the fact that some kids wear skinny jeans and others wear baggy jeans by saying that the difference expresses an innate natural preference for either tight-fitting or loose-fitting clothes. Jeans styles are about fashion, not function: they do not so much reflect their wearers' abilities or psychological traits as symbolize their identification with one group and their lack of identification with another. In a few years these particular styles will be passé, and kids will be using a different difference to announce their social allegiances.

Linguistic styles do not change as fast as clothing styles, but they too are symbols of group membership. In the case of men and women, though, the way this works is complex. Gender differences in speech are not always the result of language being used directly to symbolize the speakers' gender. Often they arise as the indirect result of speakers using language to symbolize their other social allegiances.

✴ Jocks and burnouts

Before she turned her attention to the pre-adolescents we met in Chapter 4, the sociolinguist Penelope Eckert studied older students in a suburban high school just outside Detroit. At this school as in many US high schools, students' social life was organized around a contrast between two groups known as 'jocks' and 'burnouts'.[3]

Jocks are students who embrace the middle-class values of the school: they study hard in the hope of earning good grades, support or play in the school sports teams, and throw themselves enthusiastically into extra-curricular activities like organizing dances and representing their classes on the student council. Burnouts, on the other hand, do not have middle-class aspirations and their lives do not revolve around the school: they are more drawn to the culture of the neighbouring city.

There are many ways to tell jocks and burnouts apart. They dress differently, hang out in different parts of the school, and unsurprisingly, they also speak differently. Detroit is one of a number of US cities where the pronunciation of certain vowel sounds is in the process of changing (linguists call this change 'the Northern Cities Vowel Shift'). Among speakers who have adopted the new pronunciations, the word *lunch* sounds more like *lonch*, and *cod* sounds a bit like *cad*. When Eckert analysed the frequency of these vowel sounds in the speech of high school students, she found that the contrast between old and new pronunciations was connected to their group allegiances. The jocks were more conservative in sticking to the older pronunciations, whereas the city-oriented burnouts made more use of the newer vowel sounds. But there was also a gender difference: in each group, it was the girls who were the heaviest users of the pronunciations that symbolized group identity.

Eckert's explanation is grounded in her detailed observations of high school social life. Boys, she says, gain status among their peers by demonstrating accomplishment in the activities that are valued by the group. Among jocks, for instance, boys who excel in sports are accorded high status. Burnouts respect tough boys who can hold their own in a fight. For girls, by contrast, accomplishment is not the measure of individual worth. There are jock girls who are talented athletes and burnout girls who are good fighters, but these abilities do not earn them the same credit a similarly accomplished boy would get. Girls' status among their peers is determined more by appearance, personality, and the status of the boys they date.

It may not be immediately obvious what this has to do with girls' more extreme use of the vowel pronunciations that symbolize jock or burnout identity. But Eckert's argument is that girls are impelled by their more marginal position in the group to make more intensive use of symbolic resources generally. They cannot assert their status as 'good jocks' and 'good burnouts' in the same way as boys, through action: consequently they are driven to display their commitment to the group through close attention to the symbols of jock or burnout style, such as clothing styles and vowel pronunciations. (There is a parallel here with the women MPs discussed in Chapter 7, who stick more closely than men to the rules of Parliamentary debate to symbolize their knowledge of and respect for the institution.)

In Eckert's study, jock girls were the most conservative group linguistically while burnout girls were the most innovative. The idea that women are more conservative speakers than men is a popular stereotype, and is commonly explained as a reflection of women's naturally more cautious or conformist mentality. But that account is obviously inadequate if there are just as many women whose behaviour is more innovative than that of their male peers. Many studies have found that to be the case: among adults as well as adolescents, women are typically at the extremes of both conservatism and innovation. The real generalization is not 'women are more conservative than men' or 'women are more innovative than men', but 'women carry the general tendency of their group, be that conservatism or innovation, to greater lengths than men'.

Why should women be more extreme? In Eckert's view, their speech reflects their understanding that they are judged more by style than by achievement. If any 'natural' tendency is manifested in this behaviour, it is one that both sexes share: the tendency to invest most effort where you will reap the greatest rewards.

✦ 'Mallspeak'

In Chapter 4 I reproduced part of a conversation among five young men which contained numerous utterances like these:

> you know *like* those shorts women volleyball players wear?
> he's got to *like* have his legs exposed at all times
> he's *like* at home combing his leg hairs

This way of using the word *like* is associated with younger speakers, and is often criticized by older ones on the grounds that it adds nothing to the message, but merely makes the messenger sound inarticulate. In 1999, several elite colleges in the US state of Massachusetts made headlines by announcing a drive to eliminate it from students' speech.[4] The colleges concerned included Smith and Mount Holyoke, both historically all-female institutions. That probably was not a coincidence. Although I have taken my own examples from the speech of young men, public criticism of *like* tends to associate it primarily with young women. It is one of a larger collection of verbal bad habits for which the media have coined the disparaging label 'mallspeak'.

The reference to shopping malls links the style being criticized to a particular kind of young woman, who is not unlike the Japanese *teyo/dawa* girl: she is shallow, materialistic, and only interested in trivial pursuits like shopping and hanging out with her friends at the mall. Apart from saying *like* all the time, the mallspeak girl makes excessive use of 'y'know', 'I mean', and the rising intonation pattern known as 'uptalk', which makes everything sound—y'know—like a question? Her parents and teachers are worried that the way she talks will have a negative effect on her grades and her career prospects.

These worries are reminiscent of Robin Lakoff's concerns about 'women's language' in the 1970s.[5] Lakoff interpreted both tag questions and rising intonation on statements as implying insecurity and lack of confidence: the speaker turns everything into a question because she feels unable simply to assert a fact or an opinion. This has also been the popular wisdom in more recent discussions of uptalk. But research suggests that this wisdom may have more to do with our stereotypes of young women than it does with the meaning of rising intonation.

The linguist Cynthia McLemore analysed the intonation patterns used by young women in a Texas college sorority. She found that the rising intonation pattern was used frequently (often by sorority members in positions of authority), and that it had several potential meanings. In announcements at sorority meetings, for example, it was often used to highlight new information, as opposed to information which members could be expected to know already. Whereas a reminder about a regular event in the sorority's calendar would typically be produced with falling intonation, news of a one-off event was more likely to be produced with rising intonation. The implication of the uptalk pattern was not so much a deferential 'is that OK with you?' as a rather more assertive 'pay attention'.[6]

In another study, 300 men and women of varying ages were observed ordering drinks during a university parents' weekend. The guests were asked by the server to give their name (which in this context would be new information); the observer noted whether or not the name was produced with rising intonation. The people who used rising intonation most turned out to be middle-aged men.[7]

It seems then that uptalk is neither a sign of insecurity nor the sole preserve of female speakers. *Like* is not a specifically female usage either. In Penelope Eckert's Detroit study, jock girls were the heaviest users of *like*, using it significantly more than jock boys, but there was no gender difference among the burnouts. So why is there such a widespread belief that these features are expressions of airheaded girliness?

People are probably not wrong to think that, overall, women use the features more than men (though the jock and burnout study shows that it is not all women, but only some groups of women whose heavy usage produces this impression). But the statistical association with female speakers does not license the conclusion that what the features express is femaleness, or some stereotypically female quality like insecurity or deference. 'Mallspeak' forms are innovations; and as we have just seen, if a group has adopted an innovative form it will usually be the women in the group who are in the lead. They are not doing something completely different from the men, but carrying the tendency of the whole group to a greater extreme.

This interpretation gains support from the observation that even if women use 'mallspeak' features more than men, some groups of men also use them frequently. This is true, for instance, of the young men whose conversation my own examples of *like* are taken from. However, we have already seen that these men assert a self-consciously masculine identity (as I explained in Chapter 4, their conversation is actually on the topic of how 'real men' do and don't behave). If *like* were a 'feminine' form, you would expect them to avoid it. Similarly, if the meaning of uptalk were 'I'm not really sure what I think' or 'I need your approval', then the last place you would find it would be in the speech of middle-aged professional men stating their own names.

Just because the frequency of a linguistic feature is higher in one gender's speech than in the other's, we cannot assume that it is 'about' masculinity or femininity. The adolescents in Eckert's study, for instance, were not using vowel sounds to assert their status as men and women, they were using them to assert their status as jocks and burnouts. The gender difference appeared because girls were more extreme than boys in their adherence to the norms of jock and burnout speech.

Of course, there are cases where the symbolic meaning of a linguistic feature or a style of speaking does relate primarily to masculinity or femininity. Even in these cases, though, it is a mistake to suppose that the link between language and gender is 'natural'. Speaking like a woman, or a man, is not just the automatic consequence of being one. In fact, some of the most revealing evidence about how language is conventionally used to symbolize the speaker's gender has come from studies of people whose 'real' or original gender identity does not match the one they assert in their speech.

✴ Crossing the lines

In the film *When Harry Met Sally* there is a famous scene in which Sally sets out to prove to Harry that a skilfully faked orgasm is indistinguishable from the real thing, by apparently having an orgasm as she sits at a table in a crowded New York deli. She moans, she breathes heavily, she utters words like 'yes!', 'oh, God', and 'yeah, right there'. Though Harry knows this is just a performance, it convinces the rest of the deli's clientele. At the end of the scene an older woman turns to the waitress and says, indicating Sally: 'I'll have whatever she's having.'

What Sally is exploiting is the conventional nature of communicative behaviour—the fact that certain ways of speaking, or vocalizing, can be counted on to convey certain meanings relating to the speaker's social characteristics, his or her emotional state, and even the bodily sensations he or she is experiencing. Although some of the signs which communicate orgasm are based on physiological realities (for instance, sexual arousal makes your voice breathy), they have come to function in a conventional manner, so that successful communication does not depend on the communicator's actual bodily state. You don't have to be having an orgasm to send the message that you are having one.

One group of people who make a living from this principle are phone-sex workers, whose use of language has been studied by the linguistic anthropologist Kira Hall.[8] The phone-sex line Hall's subjects worked for served a male heterosexual clientele: callers paid (by the minute) to speak to a woman who embodied their sexual fantasies. Since the medium was the phone, though, the workers did not actually have to *embody* anything: their bodies could not be seen or touched. What they did have to do was create the impression that they were the woman of the caller's dreams, using nothing but the spoken word.

Hall found that orgasms were not the only things these workers routinely faked. Many of them were not the young girls their clients were generally interested in; some of them were not heterosexual; one of them was not even a woman. Most were able to impersonate a range of 'ethnic' characters—black, Asian, Latina, southern Belle—according to the client's preference. And unsurprisingly, none of them actually felt the erotic excitement that they communicated in their performances. One woman told Hall that although she disliked the kind of client who did most of the talking himself, and just wanted her to say 'yes Master' and 'no Master', the mindlessness of these exchanges did at least allow her to get the dishes washed.

But if the way the workers come across to callers is an illusion created by the way they speak, how exactly is that illusion produced? What conventional way of speaking enables a middle-aged lesbian washing dishes in her kitchen to convince the man on the other end of the phone that she is the last word in desirable, nubile femininity?

One answer to this question turned out to be Robin Lakoff's 'women's language'. As I have already mentioned, linguists who have investigated Lakoff's claims have found that real women's speech, by and large, does not conform closely to the style she described. But the phone-sex workers made extensive use of it. One woman explained to Hall how she had learnt to prolong her calls (a valuable skill when you get paid by the minute):[9]

> I can describe myself now so that it lasts for about five minutes, by using lots of adjectives . . . and that's both—it's not just wasting time, because they need to build up a mental picture in their minds about what you look like, and also it allows me to use words that are very feminine. I always wear peach, or apricot, or black lace, or charcoal-colored lace not just black.

Adjectives and elaborate colour terms are both on Lakoff's list of women's language features. Other workers mentioned using other features discussed by Lakoff, like a 'lilting' tone and supportive questions.

Its popularity with phone-sex workers lends force to the criticism that 'women's language' is a stereotype. Phone-sex is a form of pornography, and pornography is nothing if not stereotypical. Yet the appropriateness of 'women's language' for phone-sex cannot rest simply and solely on its stereotypical association with women, for there are other stereotypes of women and their speech which could not so readily become the stuff of male fantasy—the endlessly nagging wife, for instance, or the hatchet-faced bossy schoolmarm. So what exactly is it about 'women's language' that enables it to serve the phone-sex workers' purposes?

There is a clue in Lakoff's own account. Lakoff argued that the features of 'women's language' communicate qualities which are defined as 'feminine' largely because they are hallmarks of powerlessness: politeness, self-effacement, eagerness to please. They also connote the absence of other, more powerful qualities: authority, competence, and strong opinions on anything more serious than whether an undergarment is 'peach' or 'apricot'. This subordinate and subservient femininity is a mainstream erotic taste, whereas its opposite is not. Most men do not call a sex-line hoping for an authoritative explanation of quantum mechanics or a vigorous argument about economic policy. By using 'women's language', the phone-sex workers are giving the customer what they know a lot of customers want.

Another group of people who learn to use 'women's language'—though for quite different reasons—are male-to-female (MTF) transsexuals: individuals who were born and brought up male, but who as adults seek medical assistance to become female. In the process of 'gender reassignment', their bodies will be refashioned using sex-hormones and (sometimes) surgery. But they also have to learn how to behave like women: how to move, dress, and speak in a way that will enable them to 'pass' as women in everyday social life. Many undergo speech and language therapy, and there is also a genre of self-help literature designed to address their needs.

Below is a sample of the kind of advice MTF transsexuals are given. The first extract comes from the reminiscences of someone who went through therapy, while the other two come from self-help books:

> In voice lessons I was taught to speak in a very high-pitched, very breathy, sing-song voice and to tag questions onto the end of

each sentence. And I was supposed to smile all the time when I was talking.[10]

The student learns to let her voice rise and fall as she speaks . . . A man might say, in a near monotone, 'that's a nice dress', but a woman, allowing her vocal pitch to soar, would say, 'you look gorgeous!' . . . Another good tip is to let your sentences end on an up note, almost as a question.[11]

When women talk, they move their mouths more than men; here again, smiling comes into play. . . . The more facial expression, the more smiles, the more you look and listen, the better feminine conversationalist you will be.[12]

The indebtedness of this advice to Robin Lakoff's work is obvious (though the writers have borrowed only her description of 'women's language', not her feminist critique of it). Anyone who follows it faithfully will not end up speaking like a woman, if that means 'like the average woman', or 'like most women in most everyday situations'. Most women would struggle not to feel insulted by the picture the advice paints of the 'feminine conversationalist' with her 'soaring' pitch and smiley demeanour.

But for many MTF transsexuals, the somewhat demeaning connotations of the style are probably less important than its more basic association with femaleness rather than maleness. For most people, gender is a backdrop against which they assert other kinds of status (like 'jock' or 'burnout'): it inflects everything they do, but is not usually the main thing they are trying to communicate. Transsexuals, however, will often be more explicitly concerned about communicating gender as an identity in its own right. MTFs want to pass as women, and to avoid being taken for the men they used to be. An extremely stereotypical linguistic performance of femininity is in that sense suited to their purposes: it may not be 'authentic', but it makes their gender unambiguous.

What advice do transsexuals receive who are making the opposite journey, from female to male (FTM)? According to Don Kulick, who has reviewed the expert and popular literature, the answer is 'almost none'.[13] The 'official' reason for this relates to a physiological fact. Most FTMs take testosterone, which has the effect of thickening their vocal cords and so lowering the pitch of their voices. MTFs, on the other hand, take oestrogen, which has no effect on voice-pitch. Consequently, it is often said that speech is only a problem for MTFs; FTMs do not have to worry about it.

As Kulick points out, though, this does not really explain the dearth of advice on speech for FTMs. The advice given to their MTF counterparts ranges far beyond the subject of pitch to encompass tips on smiling, speaking softly, asking questions, listening attentively, and choosing 'feminine' words like 'gorgeous'. He comments that the absence of any parallel concern among FTMs and their therapists about the fine details of male speech style

is an ideological fact as much as it is a physiological one . . . [It] reflects widespread cultural attitudes that hold that being a man is self-evident, whereas being a woman is a complicated set of procedures that require careful adherence to detailed, explicit instructions (often issued by men) about how to walk, talk, sit, eat, dress, move and display affect.[14]

Once again, it is women (or in this case, those who aspire to be women) who must pay more attention to small details of linguistic style. For men (or those who aspire to be men), very gross indicators, such as low voice-pitch, are sufficient to make them 'gender appropriate'.

Some groups of speakers manipulate the symbolic codes of gender for the express purpose of *not* being gender appropriate. One of the transsexual people I quoted earlier, describing instructions to speak in a sing-song voice, use tag questions, and smile continually, is the self-styled 'gender outlaw' Kate Bornstein. After describing her voice lessons, Bornstein goes on to say that she rejected the speech-style she was being taught. 'The teachers assumed you were going to be a heterosexual woman', she explains.[15] She herself was planning to be a lesbian, and felt that this ambition was not compatible with adopting the ultra-feminine linguistic persona symbolized by soaring pitch and smiliness.

The idea that lesbians are women who act like men (and that gay men, conversely, are men who act like women) is itself, of course, a stereotype. Like straight men and women, gay men and lesbians come in numerous varieties. Some gay and lesbian styles, however, do involve deliberate deviance from the linguistic norms of masculinity or femininity—or in some cases, the deliberate juxtaposition of masculine and feminine ways of speaking. The researcher Rusty Barrett, for instance, recorded performances by African American drag queens in Texas. The style of these performers involved mixing 'women's language' with stereotypically male ways of talking, such as obscenities and sexually explicit references.[16]

Another group of people who have been observed to switch between masculine and feminine presentations of themselves are Indian *hijras* (eunuchs), who are locally considered to belong to an intermediate 'third sex'.[17] Their language, Hindi, is one in which the grammatical marking of gender is pervasive. Any reference to a person's actions or attributes—including the speaker's own—will make clear whether the person is male or female. In most contexts *hijras* mark themselves as female, but when they talk about successful business dealings, or when they are expressing anger, they switch to masculine grammatical forms. They also use masculine forms in reference to other *hijras* to convey an attitude of great respect. This behaviour is 'deviant' in the sense that it flouts the normal expectation that a single individual will assert a single gender identity consistently. However, the switching is clearly not random: activities, emotions, and attributes are metaphorically gendered in a predictable way (for instance, business is masculine, anger is masculine, and the most venerated individuals in the group are accorded masculine status).

✦ Doing what comes culturally

It might be argued that the examples I have just been discussing are exceptional cases, which tell us nothing about the behaviour of 'normal' men and women. But it could also be argued that on the contrary, these cases where people are obviously not just 'doing what comes naturally' are very revealing about the underlying system which all of us make use of to communicate gender. Although for most of us this is not a self-conscious performance, it still depends on the cultural codes which associate certain ways of speaking with certain kinds of speakers.

It is not only in exceptional cases that speakers actively manipulate these codes. Language is part of the raw material from which we fashion our identities: many small but significant differences in the speech-styles of men and women are the results, not of pre-existing differences between the sexes, but of their unceasing efforts to *create* differences. The effort that goes into this process speaks volumes about the significance we accord to gender. But it also tells us that gendered behaviour cannot be simply 'natural', for if it were, all the effort would not be necessary.

There used to be a feminist slogan: 'If being a woman is natural, stop telling me how to do it.' For much of the last two decades we have been assailed on all sides by experts telling both women and men how it is natural for them to speak, explaining to them why they are destined to speak differently, and advising them on how to deal with the problems their differences cause (usually, by accepting what is beyond their power to change).

As I remarked in Chapter 1, there is something puzzling about this. No group of men and women in history have ever been less different, or less at the mercy of their biology, than those living in western societies today. And yet twenty-first-century westerners are drawn to a mythology which says that differences between men and women are profound and unalterable. In the final chapter of this book we must confront the question: what is it that attracts us to the myth of Mars and Venus?

9

Beyond Mars and Venus?

The idea that men and women metaphorically 'speak different languages'—that they use language in very different ways
and for very different reasons—is one of the great myths of our
time. In this book I have used research evidence in an attempt
to debunk the various smaller myths which contribute to it:
for instance, that women talk more than men (research suggests that it is commoner for men to talk more); that women's
talk is cooperative and men's is competitive (research shows
that both sexes engage in both kinds of talk); and that men and
women systematically misunderstand one another (research
has produced no good evidence that they do).

I have also emphasized certain general caveats which Mars
and Venus writers pass over in silence (or at best, make glanc-
ing reference to and then proceed to ignore). There is a great
deal of similarity between men and women, and the differences within each gender-group are typically as great as or
greater than the difference between the two. Many differences

are context-dependent: patterns which are clear in one context may be muted, non-existent, or reversed in another, suggesting that they are not direct reflections of invariant sex-specific traits.

If these points were acknowledged, the science soundbites would be headed 'Men and women pretty similar, research finds', and popular psychology books would bear titles like *There's No Great Mystery about the Opposite Sex* or *We Understand Each Other Well Enough Most of the Time*. Of course, these titles do not have the makings of best-sellers, whereas the 'men and women from different planets' story is a tried and tested formula. What does the myth of Mars and Venus do for us, that we return to it again and again?

✷ The importance of being normal

In 2003, a website calling itself 'the Gender Genie', which claimed to be able to diagnose an author's sex from a 500-word sample of their writing, became a favourite with bloggers and web-surfers. Their comments made clear that they had all done the same thing: given the Genie samples of their own writing to analyse. Obviously, they didn't need the Genie to tell them if they were male or female (which is just as well, since its error rate is very high). What they really wanted to know was how their writing measured up against the Genie's criteria for male or femaleness. One blogger, recommending the Genie to others, said: 'Go play with it: find out if you write like you're supposed to write.'[1]

The Gender Genie in fact says nothing about how men and women are supposed to write. The Genie is just a machine which has been programmed to look for certain features whose frequencies were found to differ in male- and female-authored texts in a controlled sample of written English. It counts the frequency of those features, and then delivers a guess based on the numbers. All it really tells the user is whether his or her writing supports the hypothesis that the frequency of particular features is diagnostic of a writer's sex.

Nevertheless, among the 100 bloggers whose responses I examined, all but a handful assumed that the Genie's judgement said something about them, rather than something about the Genie. Bloggers whose sex was guessed wrongly often sought reasons in their personality or life experience. One woman suggested she had been classified as male because she had been educated at a boys' school, while several others recalled that as children they had been tomboys. Men joked—sometimes with obvious unease—about the possibility that they were gay. When the Genie guessed right, by contrast, no one looked for a reason.

The bloggers' understanding of what the Gender Genie tells its users is typical of the way we approach the issue of sex-differences. We have a tendency to treat any generalization about men and women as a source of information about 'normal' male or female behaviour, which therefore has implications for how we ourselves should behave. Of course, there are some people who actively want to be different from whatever their culture defines as the norm. But for most people the desire to be normal is strong: 'am I normal?' is one of the hardy perennials of the problem-page.

For the last fifteen years, the myth of Mars and Venus has told us what is normal for men and women in the sphere of language and communication. Its generalizations about male and female language-use have come to influence our expectations about how men and women will communicate, and colour our judgements of how they do communicate. Unlike the Gender Genie, this is not just harmless fun. We see its less benign consequences when employers view women as better candidates than men for jobs that demand the ability to chat (and men as better candidates than women for jobs that demand verbal authority and directness). We see them when parents and educators expect girls to be better at languages, and boys to be better at maths. We see them when jurors at rape trials give men who claim to have 'misread a woman's signals' the benefit of the doubt. And we see them in a small way every time someone makes a joke about how much women talk or how useless men are at expressing their feelings.

✴ The importance of being different

Sex-differences fascinate us to a degree that most other biological differences don't. It is conceivable, for instance, that you could diagnose a writer's age from a sample of their prose, but no one would design a Genie for that purpose. And to my knowledge, there has never been a best-selling popular science book about the differences between right- and left-handed people.

Handedness makes an instructive comparison with sex, because it too is associated with differences in the organization of the brain. In December 2006, for instance, an article in the journal *Neuropsychology* reported that left-handed people were quicker and more efficient than right-handers at tasks like computer gaming that required the simultaneous processing of multiple stimuli.[2] If that had been a sex-difference finding, it would surely have got the same attention as the 'men have trouble listening to women' study, the 'men are better shoppers' study, and the 'women talk three times as much as men' claim. But it wasn't, and it didn't.

If handedness generates fewer soundbites than sex, that is probably because findings about it cannot be slotted into any larger narrative about the difference between right-handed and left-handed people. We don't conceive of them as different species from different planets; we don't see them as locked in an eternal 'battle of the hands'. Except perhaps in the domain of sport, we rarely think about them at all. Handedness, in short, is not significant for the organization of human *social* affairs: it does not determine a person's identity, role, or status in society. An account of how left-handers differ from right-handers would therefore lack one of the crucial ingredients which draw us to accounts of how women differ from men: it would not serve the purpose of justifying institutionalized social inequality by explaining it as the inevitable consequence of natural differences.

Is that what the myth of Mars and Venus is about? I'll let the back cover of *Why Men Don't Iron* have the first word:[3]

> Much of what is written and taught today presumes that most of the differences between women and men have been caused by society and can therefore be altered. Once this is done, men and women will become alike. And so men are challenged, pestered and lectured to change from the old dominant male to . . . get in touch with their feminine side. But what if that feminine side does not exist? . . . Men's brains are in fact wired very differently from women's, so their reactions to stimuli cannot be the same. Thus, increasing feminization of society, of food and of education is detrimental to men and eventually will be to women too.

This belongs to a time-honoured tradition of dire warnings about the dangers of altering the balance of nature by changing the relationship between men and women. Although it is contradictory (if the wiring of their brains renders all efforts to change men and women futile, how has the 'increasing feminization of society' the writers complain of been able to occur?), the political message is clear enough. We would all be better off if we reverted to the natural order in which the sexes were different and the male sex was dominant.

But as I said at the end of the last chapter, this seems an unlikely message to be sending here and now. In the societies where the myth of Mars and Venus has flourished most conspicuously, it is obvious that sex and gender differences have become less significant socially than they were in even the fairly recent past. It is also clear that many aspects of human sexual biology and reproduction are becoming more susceptible to the intervention of science and technology. 'Gender reassignment' is now done routinely; so are the procedures that enable the single, the gay and lesbian, the infertile, the post-menopausal, and sometimes even the dead to reproduce.[4] Mammals such as sheep have been cloned, bypassing the process of sexual reproduction: if we have not yet tried this with humans, it is for cultural reasons rather than because it is technically impossible.

Even our genes, where so many sex-differences allegedly reside, are no longer beyond our power to alter. Scientists did not decode the human genome just so they could sit around and marvel at it: in principle, the knowledge we now possess opens the way to all kinds of interference with nature—though as with cloning, it will be cultural considerations that determine how that knowledge can and cannot be used.

When it comes to sex and gender, then, the age-old certainties are very visibly being challenged. Meanwhile, we have developed an insatiable appetite for material which recycles the most traditional ideas imaginable about men's and women's 'natures'. Is that a contradiction—or could our uncertainty about the present and future significance of sex and gender be precisely what is enabling the myth of Mars and Venus to flourish?

★ 'A rupture in human history'

In January 2007, the *New York Times* reported one of the most significant findings of the 2005 US Census: for the first time in history, a majority of American women were not living with a spouse.[5] In Britain a month later, the Office of National Statistics revealed that the number of marriages taking place in the UK had fallen to an all-time low.[6]

A number of factors are contributing to this trend, including women marrying later, widows surviving for longer, and more couples living together but choosing not to get married. But one major factor is the choice more and more women are making not to marry, or not to remarry after divorce. They prefer independence; and today it is within their grasp. Not very long ago, most women's earnings were insufficient to maintain a household. The social price of independence was also high, since a 'respectable' woman could not have sexual relationships or children outside marriage.

The public policy scholar Alison Wolf has argued that recent changes in the position of educated middle-class women in developed societies constitute nothing less than 'a rupture in human history'.[7] In the past, Wolf notes, the lives of women in every class revolved around their domestic and reproductive roles. But in the last forty or fifty years, a combination of technological and social change has given women far more choice about how they live their lives (for instance, whether and when they have children). For an elite minority of women, the possibility now exists of leading lives which are more or less indistinguishable from the lives of their male equivalents.

That possibility has come about because of the opening up of women's previously very restricted educational and career opportunities. Wolf notes that during the first fifty years of its existence, all but a handful of the students of Somerville College (one of Oxford University's first women's colleges, founded in 1879) went on, if they had jobs, to work either in teaching (the destination of the vast majority) or in other 'caring' professions such as health and social work. This was not, as Simon Baron-Cohen might think, because the work suited their female brains, but because other professions were closed to females. When that changed, so did elite women's career choices. By the 1980s, Somerville was producing more accountants than teachers. Today, a woman graduate who remains childless can expect to rise as high and earn as much in her lifetime as a man with the same qualifications. If she has children, she can expect her lifetime earnings to be around 88 per cent of a comparable man's—not perfect equality, but closer than women have come to it before.

There have been other social changes, more difficult to measure precisely but significant nonetheless. Things my own parents treated as unbreakable rules—like men and women socializing separately (even if they were in the same pub or living room), not having opposite-sex friends, pursuing different leisure activities, and playing distinct roles within the family—are no longer rigidly adhered to. Though inequalities remain, western women have far more freedom than they once did. The sexes even look less different than they did two generations ago.

None of this is to say that gender has become irrelevant, or that men and women are now in all respects equal. Wolf stresses that outside the educated elite, economic inequalities remain very marked. Others have noted that certain problems affecting women as a group, such as the prevalence of sexual violence, may be intensifying rather than diminishing. But the sharp differentiation of the sexes which was once all-pervasive in society has weakened significantly. In their aspirations, their opportunities, their lifestyles, and their outlooks on life, educated men and women are now more similar than different.

Changes of this kind are never painless. Our ideas, our feelings, our sense of who we are, and our beliefs about what is right do not always keep pace with technological advances and changing economic conditions. This is not because our ways of thinking have been wired into our brains since the Stone Age. It is because culture is not, in fact, the superficial and ephemeral thing it is often taken for. (Conversely, as I have already pointed out, biology is not the fixed and unalterable thing it is presented as in books like *Why Men Don't Iron*.) Culture change is hard: it causes anxiety, conflict, and, in some quarters, resistance. That is why the myth of Mars and Venus has had such a warm reception from the educated western middle classes.

⭐ Change and the problem of couple communication

The target audience for Mars and Venus material is prototypically a middle-class one. Research suggests that most popular science readers have significantly higher than average levels of education.[8] Popular psychology is a more inclusive genre, but while its actual readership may not be exclusively middle class, it is middle-class lifestyles which are generally depicted in best-selling books, and periodicals aimed at a middle-class readership which are most likely to carry excerpts or features based on them. Their main theme is the difficulty middle-class men and women have communicating with one another, and the problems this causes in their relationships.

That difficulty—presented, typically, as age-old and universal —is put down to the fact that men and women inhabit separate social worlds, which give them distinctive and mutually incomprehensible ways of using and interpreting language. But that raises the question of why male–female (mis)communication does not seem to be such a problem in other societies and communities. More puzzling still, if its cause is indeed the social segregation of the sexes, the communities in which it is seen as a major issue appear to be those where there is *least* segregation.

In her classic 1962 study *Blue Collar Marriage*, the sociologist Mirra Komarovsky reported that the working-class American women she observed and interviewed did not generally expect to have extended conversations with their husbands.[9] In their community, sex-segregation was extensive: for every-day companionship and emotional support, they relied on their networks of female friends and kin. Most did not regard this as settling for second best. To them it seemed not natural, but on the contrary, rather eccentric to want your spouse to be your best friend and confidant.

This attitude is typical of traditional societies and traditional working-class communities. The ideal of 'companionate marriage', in which the partners do most things together, spend a lot of time interacting, and regard each other as friends, is essentially a modern middle-class one (though like many middle-class norms, it has gradually spread to other sections of society: Komarovsky found that women who had graduated from high school were more receptive to it than those who had not). It is made possible by the fact that middle-class men and women do not, in fact, inhabit separate social worlds (they have enough in common to sustain continuous conversation)—and it is made necessary by the fact that middle-class men and women generally do not have the close-knit, locally based networks of same-sex friends and kin that supported Komarovsky's subjects.

Today, far fewer westerners live in communities like the one described in *Blue Collar Marriage*. Economic and social changes (such as greater mobility, smaller families, and increasing rates of divorce) have weakened the bonds that held traditional families and communities together. One result has been to reduce the size of most people's support networks, making them more reliant on a small number of 'significant others'. In these conditions people expect far more from communication with their spouse or partner. When it falls short of their very high expectations, the stage is set for communication between men and women to be perceived as a serious social problem.

There are other reasons for that perception. The more similar men and women become, the more they are in direct competition for the same kinds of rewards (jobs, status, money, leisure time, personal freedom). My parents, who married in the mid-1950s, never argued about who should take out the trash, pick up groceries, wash dishes, drive the car, choose what to watch on TV, or make important financial decisions. Nor were they ever in conflict about whose job came first or whose life had to be fitted around domestic commitments. These things were settled in advance by the basic fact of gender difference. For many couples today, by contrast, pretty much everything is up for negotiation. That has the potential to lead to arguments and conflicts.

A recurring theme in Mars and Venus literature is men's allegedly underdeveloped capacity for empathy and caring. This testifies to what has not changed. When *Why Men Don't Iron* talks about an 'increasing feminization of society', that is presumably a reference to the greater visibility, status, and influence of women in domains where they were previously excluded or marginalized. But what has happened in the last forty years might be better described as an increasing *masculinization* of society, in the sense that the major shift has involved middle-class women's aspirations and attitudes becoming more like men's, focused on individual achievement and individual freedom.

Alison Wolf points out that this has led to a massive exodus of middle-class women from the engagement in paid and unpaid caring—for their families, children, the elderly, the sick, and the socially disadvantaged—which once occupied most of them for most of their lives. 'A path once followed by able women across the developed world led to university, teaching and then motherhood, homemaking and voluntary work,' says Wolf, adding: 'Such women are now too busy.'[10]

This change has not been compensated for by any reciprocal shift in men's attitudes and aspirations. Although we hear much about the so-called 'new man' with his commitment to domesticity and active parenthood (and although there is variation among men), surveys consistently find that men's contribution to both domestic work and routine forms of childcare is not much greater than it was when women were not 'too busy'.[11] Women are still doing most of the caring, but—unsurprisingly, given how much else they now do—they are more inclined to question why it should fall to them alone. That is another source of conflict in contemporary male–female relationships.

Elite women can and often do resolve the problem by contracting out what is still regarded as 'their' work to less privileged women—paid nannies, cleaners, and carers. Something that cannot easily be contracted out, however, is the task of caring for a spouse's or partner's emotional needs. It is not a coincidence that one of the key issues Mars and Venus books address is women's complaint that 'I take care of his feelings, but he doesn't take care of mine'.

The genius of the myth of Mars and Venus is to acknowledge the problems and conflicts many people are now experiencing as a result of social change, while explaining those problems and conflicts in a way that implies they have nothing to do with social change. They are as old as humanity (quite literally, in some versions of the myth) and their root cause is the irreducible natural difference between the sexes. The solution, it follows, is to do nothing: we should accept what cannot be altered, and suppress any urge to apportion blame.

In Chapter 5 I pointed out one major problem with this: in practice it tends to result in women being made responsible for ensuring that communication flows smoothly. Once again, 'personal stuff' is assumed to be women's business rather than the business of both sexes equally. But another thing that is wrong with it is that this isn't just personal stuff: these problems are symptomatic of deeper social dislocations. The belief that they are timeless, natural, and inevitable stops us thinking about what social arrangements might work better than our present ones in a society that can no longer be run on the old assumptions about what men and women do.

When the myth of Mars and Venus emphasizes that our modern problems are caused by our age-old natural differences, it is by implication saying that nothing important has changed between men and women. However similar they appear on the surface—getting the same education, doing the same jobs, earning the same money, and seeking out the same pleasures—at a deeper level, in their minds, or their brains, they are still fundamentally different. That too is reassuring to many people, because, as I said before, culture change is hard. Most of us do not especially like change, period. And even if gender no longer determines our life experiences to the extent it once did, it remains an important part of our identities, our social lives, and our sexual lives. We may not want to return to the traditional arrangement between the sexes, but that does not mean we want to live in a world where the difference between men and women is no more significant than whether someone is right- or left-handed.

✬ None of the above

Changes in male–female relations are more troubling to some people than others. For a certain kind of conservative, the weakening of traditional sex distinctions and hierarchies has become the main focus for anxiety or rage about the state of the modern world. The most obvious illustration is the rise of new forms of religious fundamentalism which are obsessed with the policing of sex and of women. But some kinds of contemporary Darwinism could well be analysed in similar terms (ironically, given that Darwin is up there with feminism on the fundamentalist's hit-list). A certain kind of Darwinian advocates obedience to nature's law as zealously as the religious fundamentalist preaches obedience to God's commandments—and he or she is usually obsessed with sex and gender too.

The resurgence of the idea that most differences between men and women are biological—and therefore, as *Why Men Don't Iron* puts it, 'unalterable'—is a striking feature of contemporary debates. Many feminists, and other liberals of the 1960s generation, thought this particular kind of sexism, based on biological determinism, had disappeared from the mainstream for good, and are alarmed by its sudden return to fashion.

In *The Blank Slate*, Steven Pinker argues that their concerns are unwarranted: we can talk about biological sex-differences without compromising our commitment to gender equality. 'The case against bigotry', he says, 'is not a factual claim that humans are biologically indistinguishable: it is a moral stance which condemns judging *individuals* according to the average traits of certain *groups*.'[12]

This is all well and good, but perhaps a little disingenuous. What Pinker is overlooking is the point I made before, that not all biological differences matter to us in the same way. People don't usually come to the subject of sex-differences as 'blank slates'. They come with an agenda: they are looking to biology to justify certain views about society—how it is and how it should be. Though Pinker himself is an exception, most people are susceptible to the argument that if a difference between men and women has a biological basis, it is inevitable ('you can't argue with nature'), desirable ('what's natural is good'), and the world should be organized around it.

Even so, I would not want to argue that 'nature' versions of the myth of Mars and Venus are axiomatically more objectionable than 'nurture' versions. That would be to reinforce the simplistic idea that biology is destiny, and to overlook how much the two versions have in common. We should not be giving a free pass to sexist arguments merely because they are couched in the language of social science, or therapy, rather than the language of genes and brain-wiring. Given a choice between the biological determinism of *Why Men Don't Iron*, the cultural determinism of *You Just Don't Understand*, and the

New Age psychobabble of *Men Are from Mars, Women Are from Venus*, our answer should be 'none of the above'.

In any case, arguing about whether a difference between men and women is biologically based or culturally constructed is pointless if the difference in question does not exist. Many Mars and Venus generalizations fall into that category. When the infamous 'women talk three times as much as men' claim hit the headlines in 2006, I spent days being asked by journalists whether I thought women's chattiness, or men's taciturnity, reflected social influences, innate characteristics, or a mixture of the two. Again, the answer is 'none of the above': the answer is that women don't talk three times as much as men.

In this argument, the feminist trump-card should be the evidence produced by research investigating the way real men and women really use language to communicate. One of the things I hope this book has shown is that the research done by linguists, anthropologists, and others—by now, a significant body of work—deserves more attention than it generally gets. What it tells us about language, about men and women, about other times and places, and about the changes affecting our own, is far more interesting and thought-provoking than the familiar Mars and Venus platitudes.

If we want real understanding to take the place of mythology, we need to reject trite formulas and sweeping claims about male and female language-use. Popular wisdom may say these claims are true, but the evidence says they are not. The evidence is more in line with what it says on a postcard someone once sent me: 'Men are from Earth. Women are from Earth. Deal with it.' Clinging to myths about the way men and women communicate is no way to deal with it. To deal with the problems and the opportunities facing men and women now, we must look beyond the myth of Mars and Venus.

Notes

Chapter 1

1. Deborah Tannen, *You Just Don't Understand: Men and Women in Conversation* (New York: Morrow, 1990); John Gray, *Men Are from Mars, Women Are from Venus* (New York: HarperCollins, 1992).

2. Anne Moir and David Jessel, *Brain Sex: The Real Difference between Men and Women* (New York: Delta Books, 1991); Deborah Blum, *Sex on the Brain: The Biological Differences between Men and Women* (New York: Penguin, 1997); Simon Baron-Cohen, *The Essential Difference: Men, Women and the Extreme Male Brain* (London: Allen Lane, 2003); Anne Moir and Bill Moir, *Why Men Don't Iron: The Fascinating and Unalterable Differences between Men and Women* (New York: Citadel, 1999).

3. Baron-Cohen, *Essential Difference*, 11.

4. Steven Pinker, *The Blank Slate: The Modern Denial of Human Nature* (London: Allen Lane, 2002), 351.

5. Quoted in Melissa Tyler and Steve Taylor, 'Come Fly with Us: Emotional Labour and the Commodification of Difference in the Airline Industry', Paper delivered at the International Labour Process Conference, Edinburgh, 1997, p. 10.

6. Baron-Cohen, *Essential Difference*, 185.

7. Ibid. 184.

8. Alon Gratch, *If Men Could Talk: Unlocking the Secret Language of Men* (New York: Little, Brown, 2001).

9. Robin Lakoff, *Language and Woman's Place* (New York: Harper & Row, 1975).

10. These findings are discussed in John F. Dovidio, 'Stereotypes', *Cambridge Encyclopedia of Language Sciences* (Cambridge: Cambridge University Press, 2007).

11. *ABC NewsOn-Line*, 17 August 2005.

12. It is only fair to record that this is not what the researchers themselves said: in fact, they were unhappy about the way their study was reported.

13. Louann Brizendine, *The Female Brain* (New York: Morgan Road, 2006).

14. For anyone wondering what the true figures are, the answer is that it's impossible to say: there is too much variation for an average to mean anything. How much people talk largely depends on what they are doing and with whom. A housebound elderly woman who rarely has visitors might utter very few words per day, while a young man who works in telesales and has a busy social life might utter a very large number. The *Guardian* newspaper conducted an experiment in which they recorded two of their journalists, one male and one female, who spent the day doing broadly similar things (see 'Do Women Really Talk More?', *Guardian*, 27 November 2006). Not much can be concluded from observations made on a single day with a sample of just two people, but for the record, the woman's word-count was 12,329 and the man's was 11,279.

15. Mark Liberman, 'Sex on the Brain', *Boston Globe*, 24 September 2006.

Chapter 2

1. Extracts from *Woman's Own* quoted in Laura Tokha, ' "I suggest you accept everything": *Woman's Own* Agony Columns in 1950, 1970 and 1990' (University of Tampere, 1993).

2. Quoted in Richard Bailey, *Images of English: A Cultural History of the Language* (Cambridge: Cambridge University Press, 1992), 253.

3. Anon., *An Essay in Defence of the Female Sex* (London: Roper & Wilkinson, 1697), 57–8.

4. Otto Jespersen, 'The Woman', repr. in Deborah Cameron (ed.), *The Feminist Critique of Language* (London: Routledge, 1998), 233.

5. Ibid. 234.

6. Ibid. 236.

7. Ibid. 238.

8. Theodore Zeldin, *Conversation: How Talk Can Change Your Life* (London: Harvill Press, 1998), 94.

9. Alexander Chamberlain, 'Women's Languages', *American Anthropologist*, 14 (1912), 579–81.

10. Paul Furfey, 'Men's and Women's Language', *American Catholic Sociological Review*, 5 (1944), 218.

11. Tok Pisin is the English-based pidgin which is the national language of Papua New Guinea.

12. These insults were originally delivered in a mixture of Tok Pisin and the indigenous language Taiap: the English translation is Don Kulick's. See Don Kulick, 'Speaking as a Woman: Structure and Gender in Domestic Arguments in a New Guinea Village', *Cultural Anthropology*, 8/4 (1993), 522.

13. Don Kulick, *Language Shift and Cultural Reproduction* (Cambridge: Cambridge University Press, 1992), 119.

14. Elinor Ochs Keenan, 'Norm-Makers, Norm-Breakers: Uses of Speech by Men and Women in a Malagasy Community', in Richard Bauman and Joel Sherzer (eds.), *Explorations in the Ethnography of Speaking* (Cambridge: Cambridge University Press, 1974), 137.

15. Joel Sherzer, 'A Diversity of Voices: Men's and Women's Speech in Ethnographic Perspective', in Susan Phillips, Susan Steele, and Christine Tanz (eds.), *Language, Gender and Sex in Comparative Perspective* (Cambridge: Cambridge University Press, 1987), 119.

16. *Observer*, 4 May 1997.

17. *Working Woman*, September 1990, pp. 216–17.

Chapter 3

1. Janet Shibley Hyde, 'The Gender Similarities Hypothesis', *American Psychologist*, 60/6 (2005), 581–92.

2. Janet Shibley Hyde and Marcia Linn, 'Gender Differences in Verbal Ability: A Meta-Analysis', *Psychological Bulletin*, 104 (1988), 53–69.

3. J. K. Chambers, *Sociolinguistic Theory* (Oxford: Blackwell, 1995), 136.

4. Quoted in 'Do Women Really Talk More?', *Guardian*, 27 November 2006, G2, p. 7.

5. Robin Lakoff, *Language and Woman's Place* (New York: Harper & Row, 1975).

6. Janet Holmes, 'Hedging Your Bets and Sitting on the Fence: Some Evidence for Tag Questions as Support Structures', *Te Reo*, 27 (1984), 47–62.

7. See Deborah Cameron, Fiona McAlinden, and Kathy O'Leary, 'Lakoff in Context: The Form and Function of Tag Questions', in Jennifer Coates and Deborah Cameron (eds.), *Women in Their Speech Communities* (London: Longman, 1988).

8. Pamela Fishman, 'Interaction: The Work Women Do', in Barrie Thorne, Cheris Kramarae, and Nancy Henley (eds.), *Language, Gender and Society* (Rowley, Mass.: Newbury House, 1983).

9. Deborah Tannen, *You Just Don't Understand* (New York: Morrow, 1990).

10. Simon Baron-Cohen, *The Essential Difference* (London: Allen Lane, 2003).

11. Anne Moir and Bill Moir, *Why Men Don't Iron* (New York: Citadel, 1999).

Chapter 4

1. Quoted in Penelope Eckert, 'Cooperative Competition in Adolescent "Girl Talk"', in Deborah Tannen (ed.), *Gender and Conversational Interaction* (New York: Oxford University Press, 1993), 32.

2. Deborah Tannen, *You Just Don't Understand* (New York: Morrow, 1990), 43–4.

3. Ibid. 47.

4. Judith Baxter, '"Do We Have to Agree with Her?" How High School, Girls Negotiate Leadership in Public Contexts', in Baxter (ed.), *Speaking Out: The Female Voice in Public Contexts* (Basingstoke: Palgrave, 2005), 164, 170.

5. Ibid. 166.

6. Ibid. 169.

7. Ibid. 168.

8. Ibid. 173.

9. Marjorie Harness Goodwin, *The Hidden Life of Girls: Games of Stance, Status and Exclusion* (Malden, Mass.: Blackwell, 2006).

10. Ibid. 1.

11. Penelope Eckert, 'Vowels and Nail Polish: The Emergence of Linguistic Style in the Preadolescent Heterosexual Market', in Deborah Cameron and Don Kulick (eds.), *The Language and Sexuality Reader* (London: Routledge, 2006), 190.

12. Ibid. 191.

13. Eckert, 'Cooperative Competition', 33.

14. Adapted from Deborah Cameron, 'Performing Gender Identity: Young Men's Talk and The Construction of Heterosexual Masculinity', in Sally Johnson and Ulrike Meinhof (eds.), *Language and Masculinity* (Oxford: Blackwell, 1997), 53-4.

15. Robin Dunbar, *Grooming, Gossip and the Evolution of Language* (London: Faber, 1996).

16. Terttu Nevalainen and Helena Raumolin-Brunberg, *Historical Sociolinguistics* (London: Longman, 2003).

17. Tannen, *You Just Don't Understand*, 47.

Chapter 5

1. John Gray, *Men Are from Mars, Women Are from Venus* (New York: HarperCollins, 1992), 59.

2. John J. Gumperz, *Discourse Strategies* (Cambridge: Cambridge University Press, 1982).

3. Daniel Maltz and Ruth Borker, 'A Cultural Approach to Male–Female Misunderstanding', in John J. Gumperz (ed.), *Language and Social Identity* (Cambridge: Cambridge University Press, 1982).

4. Helen Reid-Thomas, 'The Use and Interpretation by Men and Women of Minimal Responses in Informal Conversation', M. Litt. thesis, Strathclyde University, 1993.

5. '10 Classic Career Mistakes All Women Make', *Options*, February 1992.

6. Gray, *Men from Mars, Women from Venus*, 250-1.

7. For a full analysis see Susan Ehrlich, *Representing Rape* (London: Routledge, 2002). Extracts from tribunal proceedings reproduced in

this chapter are taken from Susan Ehrlich, 'The Discursive Reconstruction of Sexual Consent', in Deborah Cameron and Don Kulick (eds.), *The Language and Sexuality Reader* (London: Routledge, 2006), 196–214.

8. Judgement, 'In the Matter of M. A.', quoted in Ehrlich, 'Discursive Reconstruction of Sexual Consent', 210.

9. Celia Kitzinger and Hannah Frith, 'Just Say No: The Use of Conversation Analysis in Developing a Feminist Perspective on Sexual Refusal', *Discourse & Society*, 10/3 (1999), 293–316.

10. Ibid. 310–11.

11. Deborah Tannen, *You Just Don't Understand* (New York: Morrow, 1990), 298.

Chapter 6

1. Jonathan Prynn, 'Men Are Better at Shopping than Women: It's in the Genes', *Evening Standard*, 6 October 2005.

2. Ibid.

3. Anne Moir and Bill Moir, *Why Men Don't Iron* (New York: Citadel, 1999).

4. Simon Baron-Cohen, *The Essential Difference* (London: Allen Lane, 2003).

5. Jeannette McGlone, 'Sex Differences in the Cerebral Organization of Verbal Functions in Patients with Unilateral Brain Lesions', *Brain*, 100 (1977), 775–93.

6. *Neuroreport*, 9/12 (24 August 1998), 2803–7.

7. Robin Dunbar, *Grooming, Gossip and the Evolution of Language* (London: Faber, 1996).

8. Rhawn Joseph, 'The Evolution of Sex Differences in Language, Sexuality and Visual-Spatial Skills', *Archives of Sexual Behavior*, 29/1 (2000), 35–66.

9. See Frances Dahlberg (ed.), *Woman the Gatherer* (New Haven: Yale University Press, 1981); Richard Lee and Richard Daly (eds.), *The Cambridge Encyclopaedia of Hunters and Gatherers* (Cambridge: Cambridge University Press, 1999).

10. Dunbar, *Grooming*.

11. Geoffrey F. Miller, 'Sexual Selection for Cultural Displays', in R. Dunbar, C. Knight, and C. Power (eds.), *The Evolution of Culture* (Edinburgh: Edinburgh University Press, 1999), 71–91.

12. Geoffrey F. Miller, *The Mating Mind: How Sexual Choice Shaped the Evolution of Human Nature* (New York: Doubleday, 2000).

13. See Terttu Nevalainen and Helena Raumolin-Brunberg, *Historical Sociolinguistics* (London: Longman, 2003) for examples from early modern England.

14. Dale Spender, *Man Made Language* (London: Routledge & Kegan Paul, 1980).

Chapter 7

1. Andrew Rawnsley, 'Gordon Brown Is from Mars; David Cameron Is from Venus', *Observer*, 19 November 2006.

2. Aurora, *Managing Gender Capital* (British American Tobacco, 2002).

3. Patricia Manning with Marilyn Haddock, *Leadership Skills for Women: Achieving Impact as a Manager* (California: Crisp Publications, 1989), 7.

4. Cynthia Berryman-Fink, 'Gender Issues: Management Style, Mobility and Harassment', in Peggy Y. Byers (ed.), *Organizational Communication* (Needham Heights, Mass.: Allyn and Bacon, 1997), 269.

5. Quoted in Judith Mattson Bean, 'Gaining a Public Voice: A Historical Perspective on American Women's Public Speaking', in Judith Baxter (ed.), *Speaking Out* (Basingstoke: Palgrave, 2005), 26.

6. Sylvia Shaw, 'Governed by the Rules? The Female Voice in Parliamentary Debates', in Baxter (ed.), *Speaking Out*.

7. Joni Lovenduski, Margaret Moran, and Boni Sones, 'Whose Secretary Are You, Minister?' (Research report, 2004).

8. Clare Walsh, *Gender and Discourse: Language and Power in Politics, the Church and Organizations* (London: Longman, 2002).

9. Adapted from Janet Holmes, *Gendered Talk in the Workplace* (Oxford: Blackwell, 2006), 57–8. The transcription of this and the following examples has been modified slightly to make it easier to read.

10. Ibid. 56.

11. Ibid. 165.

12. Adapted from Lanita Jacobs-Huey, *From the Kitchen to the Parlor: Language and Becoming in African American Women's Hair Care* (New York: Oxford University Press, 2006), 35.

13. Bonnie McElhinny, 'Challenging Hegemonic Masculinities: Female and Male Police Officers Handling Domestic Violence', in Kira Hall and Mary Bucholtz (eds.), *Gender Articulated: Language and the Socially Constructed Self* (London: Routledge, 1995).

14. See Deborah Cameron, 'Styling the Worker', in *On Language and Sexual Politics* (London: Routledge, 2006).

15. Holmes, *Gendered Talk*, 35.

Chapter 8

1. The information in this section is taken from Momoko Nakamura, 'Creating Indexicality: Schoolgirl Speech in Meiji Japan', in Deborah Cameron and Don Kulick (eds.), *The Language and Sexuality Reader* (London: Routledge, 2006), 270–84.

2. Mary Bucholtz, ' "Why Be Normal?" Language and Identity Practices in a Community of Nerd Girls', *Language and Society*, 28/2 (1999), 203–23.

3. Penelope Eckert, *Jocks and Burnouts: Social Categories and Identity in the High School* (New York: Teachers Press, 1989).

4. Kate Zernike, 'Talk is like, you know, cheapened: colleges introduce classes to clean up campus "mallspeak" ', *Boston Globe*, 31 January 1999.

5. Robin Lakoff, *Language and Woman's Place* (New York: Harper & Row, 1975).

6. Cynthia McLemore, 'The Pragmatic Interpretation of English Intonation: Sorority Speech', Ph.D. diss., University of Texas, Austin, 1991.

7. Cited by Penelope Eckert, 'Language and Gender in Adolescence', in Janet Holmes and Miriam Meyerhoff (eds.), *The Handbook of Language and Gender* (Malden, Mass.: Blackwell, 2003), 395.

8. Kira Hall, 'Lip Service on the Fantasy Lines', in Kira Hall and Mary Bucholtz (eds.), *Gender Articulated* (London: Routledge, 1995), 183–216.

9. Ibid. 199–200.

10. Kate Bornstein, interview with Shannon Bell, in Arthur Kroker and Marilouise Kroker, *The Last Sex: Feminism and Outlaw Bodies* (New York: St Martins Press, 1993), 104–20.

11. Veronica Vera, *Miss Vera's Finishing School for Boys Who Want to Be Girls* (New York: Doubleday, 1997), 131–2.

12. Jennifer Anne Stevens, *From Masculine to Feminine and All Points in between: A Practical Guide* (Cambridge, Mass.: Different Path, 1990), 76–7.

13. Don Kulick, 'Transgender and Language: A Review of the Literature and Suggestions for the Future', *GLQ* 5 / 4 (1999), 605–22.

14. Ibid. 609.

15. Bornstein, interview with Shannon Bell.

16. Rusty Barrett, 'Supermodels of the World, Unite!', in Cameron and Kulick (eds.), *Language and Sexuality Reader*, 151–63.

17. Kira Hall and Veronica O'Donovan, 'Shifting Gender Positions among Hindi-Speaking Hijras', in Victoria Bergvall, Janet Bing, and Alice Freed (eds.), *Rethinking Language and Gender Research* (London: Longman 1996), 251–5.

Chapter 9

1. See Deborah Cameron, 'Dreaming of Genie: Language, Gender Difference and Identity on the Web', in Sally Johnson and Astrid Ensslin (eds.), *Language in the Media* (London: Continuum, in press).

2. 'Left-Handers Think More Quickly', *BBC News Online*, 6 December 2006.

3. Anne Moir and Bill Moir, *Why Men Don't Iron* (New York: Citadel, 1999).

4. I am referring to the occasional instances where sperm has been taken from a man before his death and frozen for later use by his surviving partner, who is enabled to become pregnant by artificial insemination or in-vitro fertilization.

5. '51% of women are now living without spouse', *New York Times*, A1, 16 January 2007.

6. 'Marriages Decrease', *National Statistics Online*, 21 February 2007.

7. Alison Wolf, 'Working Girls', *Prospect Magazine*, 121, April 2006.

8. See e.g. Suzana Herculano-Houzel, 'What does the public want to know about the brain?', Letters to the Editor, *Nature Neuroscience*, 6 (2003), 325. This researcher found that almost 90 per cent of her sample, made up of people who had sought out information about the brain from popular sources, were graduates.

9. Mirra Komarovsky, *Blue Collar Marriage* (New York: Vintage, 1962).

10. Wolf, 'Working Girls'.

11. According to the UK Office of National Statistics, British women on average do 3 hours of housework a day to men's 1 hour 40 minutes (this figure excludes shopping and childcare, of which men also do less). A supplementary note to the authors of *Why Men Don't Iron*: 60 per cent of men do, in fact, iron. For women, the figure is over 90 per cent. However, both sexes identify ironing as the domestic task they dislike most. I would therefore provisionally interpret the sex-difference in ironing-frequency not as evidence of some innate masculine aversion to chores which women's brain-wiring gives them a predilection for, but as a consequence of the fact that fewer women than men can get someone else to do their ironing for them.

12. Steven Pinker, *The Blank Slate* (London: Allen Lane, 2002), 145.

Index

Index

Index

Index